D0142930

PHILOSOPHY AND THEOLOGY IN THE MIDDLE AGES

In the first Christian centuries being a philosopher was still a practical alternative to being a Christian. Philosophical systems offered intellectual, practical and moral codes for living. Yet by the Middle Ages in the West and the Orthodox East philosophy was largely incorporated into Christian belief. From the end of the Roman Empire to the Reformation and Renaissance of the sixteenth century Christian theologians had a virtual monopoly on higher education. The complex interaction between theology and philosophy, which was the result of the efforts of Christian leaders and thinkers to assimilate the most sophisticated ideas of science and secular learning into their own system of thought, is the subject of this book.

Augustine, as the most widely read author in the Middle Ages is the starting-point. Dr Evans then discusses the definitions of philosophy and theology and the classical sources to which the medieval scholar would have had access when studying philosophy and its theological implications. Part I ends with an analysis of the problems of logic, language and rhetoric. In Part II the sequence of topics – God, cosmos, man – follows the outline of the *summa*, or systematic course in theology, which developed from the twelfth century as a textbook framework.

Does God exist? What is he like? What are human beings? Is there a purpose to their lives? These are the great questions of philosophy and religion and the issues to which the medieval theologian addressed himself. From 'divine simplicity' to ethics and politics, this book is a lively introduction to the debates and ideas of the Middle Ages.

G. R. Evans is University Lecturer in History at the University of Cambridge. Her publications include *Anselm* (1989), *The Thought of Gregory the Great* (1986), *Augustine on Evil* (1983) and *Alan of Lille* (1983).

9
1

Phil.
21.08

PHILOSOPHY AND THEOLOGY IN THE MIDDLE AGES

G. R. Evans

NYACK COLLEGE LIBRARY
1 South Boulevard
Nyack, NY 10960-3698

London and New York

First published 1993
by Routledge
11 New Fetter Lane, London EC4P 4EE

Simultaneously published in the USA and Canada
by Routledge
29 West 35th Street, New York, NY 10001

Reprinted 1994

© 1993 G. R. Evans

Typeset in 10/12 point Garamond by
Computerset, Harmondsworth, Middlesex
Printed in Great Britain by
T. J. Press (Padstow) Ltd, Padstow, Cornwall

All rights reserved. No part of this book may be reprinted or
reproduced or utilized in any form or by any electronic,
mechanical, or other means, now known or hereafter
invented, including photocopying and recording, or in any
information storage or retrieval system, without permission in
writing from the publishers.

British Library Cataloguing in Publication Data
Evans, G. R.
Philosophy and Theology in the Middle Ages
I. Title
189

Library of Congress Cataloging in Publication Data
Philosophy and theology in the middle ages
Evans, G. R. (Gillian Rosemary)
p.   cm.
Includes bibliographical references and index.
1.   Philosophy. Medieval.   2.   Theology, Doctrinal–History–
Middle Ages. 600–1500.   I.   Title.
B721.E86 1993
189–dc20 92–14375

ISBN 0–415–08908–5
0–415–08909–3 (pbk)

CONTENTS

CONTENTS

PREFACE

This is a book mostly about the Western tradition of study of philosophy and theology in the Middle Ages. That is partly for reasons of space. It is necessary to be heavily selective even in giving an account of this geographically limited area of growth in the relationship between philosophy and theology. But we should need to concentrate on the West in any case, because that was where the main stream of philosophical development now flowed. After the centuries which immediately followed the fall of the Roman Empire, Byzantine Christianity developed its own branch of the tradition in terms of theological scholarship. The two were not easily able to keep in touch, because few scholars knew both Greek and Latin after the sixth century; and after 1054 the Greek and Latin Churches were divided and ceased to be in communion with one another. The Byzantine style of Christian scholarship placed an emphasis on mysticism. It drew more heavily and more directly on late Platonism than the West was able to do, while the West made substantial use of Aristotle. Without diverging doctrinally except over the question of the Procession of the Holy Spirit and some lesser matters such as the use of leavened or unleavened bread in the Eucharist and whether purgatory purged by fire, the two Churches came to have subtly but undeniably different intellectual flavours. At the Council of Florence (1438–45), when a serious attempt was made to reunite the two Churches, it was dramatically evident that they spoke not only two languages, but also two languages of thought.

If we must limit ourselves to only a few glances at the Greek East, we can take in the much broader range of themes in which philosophy interested itself in our period than was the case even in the late antique world. In the twelfth century, the Canon Hugh of St Victor (c.1096–1141), who taught at Paris, made a distinction between those aspects of theology which are concerned with the being and nature of God, his unity and Trinity and the creation of the world; and those branches of the subject which depend for our knowledge of them on the revelation of Holy Scripture. The first group contains the bulk of the lively issues of philosophy-theology in the late antique and early Christian world – what Boethius in the sixth century understood by *theologia*. These issues were still very much alive in the Middle Ages, with fresh slants derived from mediaeval understanding of Aristotelian notions of 'end' and 'purpose', 'power' and 'act', 'causation', 'origin' and 'source', and of epistemology. In the middle and later thirteenth century we find theologians and those who specialised in philosophy in the universities alike busy with questions about man's knowledge of God-in-himself; the divine simplicity; ideas in the divine mind; being and essence; the eternity of the world; the nature of matter; the elements; beatitude; and such scientific practicalities as the motion of the heart. But they were also dealing, and sometimes in the same works, with grace, the Church, sacraments and so on, using philosophical categories and methods. It was chiefly out of the work done in the late mediaeval centuries on these topics that there sprang the debates of the Reformation.

No author, Christian or secular, was more widely read in the West throughout the Middle Ages than Augustine, or more influential in forming the minds of Western scholars as they sought to make sense in Latin of concepts first framed and developed in Greek. So Augustine must be our starting-point. The story begins in the present volume with the issue of the relationship between philosophy and theology which won partisans of various opinions throughout the Middle Ages. Then we come to the question of the classical sources the mediaeval scholar may have been able to use when we wanted to study philosophy in its theological implications. Part I ends with a sketch of the problems of logic and language and their epistemological roots, which arose out of the study of the grammar, logic and rhetoric of the *trivium*. These were a foundation study for all mediaeval scholars and perhaps the area in which the most penetrating new work of the Middle Ages was done. In Part II the sequence of topics broadly follows the outline of the *summa*, or systematic encyclopaedia of theology, which developed from the twelfth century as a textbook framework. The aim of this arrangement of the material is to introduce the modern reader to the mediaeval world of thought in something of the way in which the mediaeval student came to it.

ACKNOWLEDGEMENTS

This book was first written as the second volume of a series to be published in German. I am grateful to Professor Christopher Stead and Professor A. Ritter for suggesting that I write it, and to its publishers, Kohlhammer. But it has seemed that it might fill a gap in the available literature in English, too, and so, with some minor changes, it is offered here in the language in which it was first drafted.

ABBREVIATIONS

AHDLMA	*Archives d'histoire doctrinale et littéraire du moyen âge*
CCCM	*Corpus Christianorum Continuatio Medievalis*
CHLGEMP	*Cambridge History of Later Greek and Early Mediaeval Philosophy*, ed. A. H. Armstrong (Cambridge, 1970)
CHLMP	*Cambridge History of Later Mediaeval Philosophy*, ed. N. Kretzmann, A. Kenny and A. Pinborg (Cambridge, 1982)
C. Jul.	Augustine, *Against Julian*
CSEL	*Corpus Scriptorum Ecclesiasticorum Latinorum*
De Civ. Dei	Augustine, *The City of God*
De Doct. Chr.	———, *On Christian Doctrine*
De Trinitate	———, *On the Trinity*
De Vera Religione	———, *On True Religion*
GP	Gilbert of Poitiers, *Commentaries on Boethius*, ed. N. M. Häring (Toronto, 1966)
Huygens	T. Huygens, *Accessus ad Auctores* (Leiden, 1970)
'I divieti'	M. Grabmann, 'I divieti ecclesiastici di Aristotele sotto Innocenzio Ill e Gregorio IX', *Miscellanea Historiae Pontificiae*, 7 (Rome, 1941)
K	*Grammatici Latini*, ed. H. Keil (8 vols, Leipzig, 1855–80)
Lafleur	C. Lafleur, ed., *Quatre introductions à la philosophie au xiiiᵉ siècle* (Montreal/Paris, 1988)
Lottin	O. Lottin, *Psychologie et morale aux xiiᵉ et xiiiᵉ siècles*, V (Gembloux, 1959)
PG	*Patrologia Graeca*
PL	*Patrologia Latina*
S	Anselm of Canterbury, *Opera Omnia*, ed. F. S. Schmitt (Rome/Edinburgh, 1938–69)
TC	Thierry of Chartres, *Commentaries on Boethius*, ed. N. M. Häring (Toronto, 1971)

Part I

1

PHILOSOPHY AND THEOLOGY

THE IDEA OF PHILOSOPHY

Christians who spoke of 'philosophy' did not mean the same thing in the fifth century as they were to do a thousand years later. Mediaeval readers were drawing upon much the same body of textbooks as were already regarded as the classics of the subject in Augustine's time. But they no longer lived in a world where 'being a philosopher' was a practical alternative to being a Christian, and where one might meet and talk with men who had made that choice. Philosophy in the Middle Ages was largely an academic study, and chiefly confined in its scope to those themes and topics on which the surviving ancient textbooks provided some teaching. It was a live and growing discipline, but no longer in quite the same way as it had been in the first Christian centuries, when rival schools and factions sprang up and died away, and the enterprising were constantly trying out new permutations of Platonist, Aristotelian and Stoic ideas. That is not to say that the mediaevals did not do significant new work in philosophy. But they did so, as it were, piecemeal, pushing forward frontiers at particular points, and not as a rule in ways creative of new systems of life and thought.

The philosophical systems known to Augustine were not only intellectual but also practical and moral. They were in general designed to lead the adherent through the course of his life in virtue, towards a goal of happiness (Aristotle making the *telos*, or purpose, happiness, the Stoics tending to see virtue as an end in itself). Augustine had read Varro's (now lost) book of 288 possible philosophies (*De Civ. Dei* XIX.i.2). They all, he observes, set the *beata vita* or 'blessed life' before mankind as the end to be attained, in one form or another. Augustine himself did not think it inappropriate to write a book *De Beata Vita* in the first months after his conversion to Christianity, in which he felt free to make use of whatever in the philosophers he found helpful, and

3

consistent with his Christian belief. It was also not uncongenial to the philosophically minded Christian to go along, at least in part, with the conception of the divine which philosophers had come to find satisfactory: emptied, as it were, of any character but those of goodness, beauty, truth, justice; sometimes of everything but pure being; sometimes even of that. It was therefore neither difficult nor intrinsically objectionable to identify such a Supreme Being with the God of the Christians. No syncretism was involved. One simply took the view that Plato, for example, had come by natural reason to that real but limited understanding of the nature of God which St Paul tells us is to be had by contemplation of his creation (Romans 1.19–20). If philosophers argued that the happy life was attained by those who aspired to rise as high as possible above their lower natures, and to imitate God in a tranquillity which turned its back on worldly lusts and worldly ambitions, Christians need have no quarrel with that. They will wish to go further. But they can take such philosophical endeavours as the companionable efforts of fellow-travellers on the same road. For those philosophers who accepted the immortality of the soul, the happy life was not confined to the present but extended, and indeed had its full realisation, beyond this life. Here again they were not necessarily at cross-purposes with Christians (although, as we shall see, there were important differences). Christianity was, in this sense, itself a philosophy.

We must move to Boethius (c.480–c.524) to pursue the theme of philosophy as the guide of life, at least in the West.[1] *The Consolation of Philosophy* remained a challenge to Christian scholars because it appears to show a Boethius, presumably Christian when he wrote the theological tractates, returning to philosophy under the pressures of political imprisonment and despair at the end of his life. In his dialogue with a Philosophia who has to be much altered before she can be identified with the Sapientia or Holy Wisdom of the Old Testament or with the Christ of the New,[2] Boethius is first led to see that he need not lose faith in the ultimate benevolent purpose and continuing power of Providence just because his own life now seems to be at the mercy of fickle Fortune. Then he is taken through a discussion of the manner in which the details of human fate may be seen to depend ultimately upon a divine and unchanging simplicity, and through an exploration of the problem of divine foreknowledge in its relation to human freedom. There is nothing in what is said which is incompatible with Boethius' remaining a Christian. But it is Philosophia who is his guide and who brings him a consolation which depends ultimately upon resignation and an intellectual grasp of the essential orderliness of what had before seemed a random and disorderly sequence of catastrophes.

Boethius' *Consolation* was read and commented upon by Carolingian authors, among them Remigius of Auxerre (c.841–c.908), who sought out what philosophy he could find in ancient texts. The *Consolation* was translated into several vernaculars in the same period. Nevertheless, it remained true that one could no longer meet a philosopher in the way that Augustine or Boethius could. There were no individuals in Western Europe after Bede's day (c.673–735) who would call themselves philosophers not Christians, who were choosing a philosophical system as a basis for a way of life in preference to Christianity (though, as we shall see, some thought it might be a guide in addition to Christianity).

This was in part the result of the major changes in cultural patterns brought about by the fall of the Roman Empire. It was no longer the case that those who ruled Europe were educated in rhetoric and philosophy. Many were illiterate, and most were more concerned with the practicalities of war and government than with patronage of learning. It fell largely to the monasteries and the cathedral schools (where clergy who were to serve the cathedral were trained) to sustain what level of scholarship they could. Bede's mentor, Benedict Biscop (c.628–89), travelled on the continent, spent some time as a monk at Lérins, and brought back from Rome, and Monte Cassino in South Italy, the manuscripts which were to lay the foundation of the libraries of the monasteries he founded at Wearmouth and Jarrow in the north of England. Bede was given into his care as a child oblate at the age of 7. He spent a productive life making the heritage of books a working part of the tradition of Western monastic life. He wrote on spelling and other *grammaticalia*; the procedure for calculating the date of Easter; the natural world (using Isidore, Suetonius and Pliny); history and biography designed to show the hand of God in human affairs; and a vast body of Scriptural commentary derived from Augustine, Jerome, Ambrose and Gregory the Great, with some reflections of his own. The character of all this was practical. Bede sought to meet the needs of his monks, to create a Christian scholarship which was useful and edifying rather than speculative, and in this he was spectacularly successful.

But the success and popularity of his works underlines the nature of the change which had taken place. One would not now meet individuals in the West who were living their lives according to a philosophical and moral system which was, although not Christian, to all intents and purposes a religion as well as a set of intellectually apprehended opinions about the universe. One could ask whether Boethius may have been as much a philosopher as a Christian in this sense. But it is not a question which could be asked of a contemporary of Bede two hundred years later. From now on, the term *philosophus* would be used in one of two ways: to refer to an individual among the ancient philosophers;[3] or to contemporaries who appeared to be adopting their methods as thinkers and going along with their ideas, although remaining themselves Christian scholars.[4] Of the first, it was possible to continue to take Augustine's view, that they were in the main good and intelligent men who had had the misfortune to be born before Christ, but who had made admirable and even useful progress towards an understanding of the truth. If some of their views had to be excluded from acceptance by Christians, that was only to be expected, and the task of Christian theological scholarship was to sift the wheat from the chaff.

Of the second, it was necessary to take a suspicious view. Here were contemporaries who called themselves Christians, arguing on grounds of reason for opinions which were not always clearly compatible with Christian orthodoxy, and indeed sometimes flagrantly contradicted it. Instances of this pejorative use of *philosophi* for the moderns are to be found from late in the eleventh century. When Gilbert Crispin, then abbot of Westminster, describes a 'philosophical society' (meeting in London), he presents us with a mystery, for no other writer of the time hints at any such thing, even as a literary fiction. Gilbert's *philosophi* were probably no more than that, for his purpose is to construct a setting in which to conduct a dialogue between a philosopher and a Christian as a pair for his dialogue between a Christian and a Jew. (There are many ways in and out of the meeting place. He needs a guide. His introductory description is full of symbolism. He has to wait outside until summoned in.)[5]

The gathering, when he enters it, is discussing, in twos and threes, not one but several questions. Some are trying to reconcile Aristotle and Porphyry on genera and species. Some are trying to determine whether grammar is a branch of logic. The debate which catches Gilbert's interest is between 'two philosophers of different sects' (*diversae sectae*), a Christian and a pagan (*gentilis*). The issue between them is the rational grounds for Christian faith, and the credit which should be given to the authority of revelation. The 'philosophical society' recedes into the background as the discussion works its way through the content of the Christian faith. We hear no more of the *litterati homines*, and in any case Gilbert makes it plain as he introduces them that they were 'as it seemed to me, students of the discipline of logic'; only in the sketchiest sense does he envisage them as like the philosophers of old.

6

Peter Abelard, a younger contemporary of Gilbert's, taught in northern France. He wrote a dialogue involving a philosopher, a Jew and a Christian, introduced this time by a dream-sequence. That in itself indicates the impossibility of finding real philosophers for the exercise. 'As is the way in dreams . . .' he begins ('*iuxta visionis modum*').[6] The main topic in the part of the dialogue between Christian and Jew is the Incarnation, which Gilbert's treatise, and perhaps Anselm of Canterbury's *Why God became man* (*Cur Deus Homo*), shows to have been currently fashionable.[7] In his discussion with the Philosopher the Christian tackles the problem of the nature of the highest Good and of *beatitudo*, and the way in which the virtues may lead to its attainment; they also consider the supreme evil, punishment and the Last Things. There are hints that Abelard had picked up from his reading some notion of the character of the ancient philosopher. His Philosopher criticises the Jews as beasts wrapped up in their senses, who need miracles to move them to faith, while philosophers seek to know the reason why; these 'Greeks seek wisdom', Abelard says.[8] There is an understanding of the search for happiness as a journey towards perfection.[9] To arrive there is to be blessed. But Abelard suffers like Gilbert from the disadvantage of never having met an individual who would call himself a philosopher as opposed to a Christian.

In the Middle Ages, then, we are, in practice, dealing with Christian thinkers who have read a little ancient philosophy, and not with those whose lives are guided by a philosophical system. Thus Abelard is reduced to comparing the results of using proofs drawn from revelation with proofs drawn exclusively from reason, rather as Gilbert does; he has to do without a live philosopher. John of Wales, Franciscan preacher of the thirteenth century, made a stout effort to describe the good philosopher, and found him much like a friar in his learning and humility.[10] Some of those teaching philosophy in the Paris Arts Faculty late in the same century were also evidently trying to revive the notion that philosophy is a way of life. In 1277 the condemned propositions included the statements (40) that there is no more excellent way of life than the philosophical and (154) that only philosophers are wise. Again, we glimpse in a thirteenth-century *accessus* or introduction to philosophy an attempt to depict philosophy as a guide of life. An introduction to the *Consolation* itself describes Boethius as showing the way philosophy can comfort in the face of human experience of the changeableness of all good things on earth, the deceptiveness of a happiness more apparent than real; we are told that he sets before us the working of providence, so that we may face with a quiet mind whatever befalls us (Lafleur, pp. 229–32).

When it came to defining philosophy in the Middle Ages, the most practical way to make clear its scope proved to be to use a *schema* which shows its place in relation to other disciplines. *Schemata* of the arts and sciences have precedents in late classical and Carolingian encyclopaedists, and in twelfth-century versions.[11] In the thirteenth century, the task was undertaken again. About 1250, Arnulfus Provincialis, Master of Arts at Paris, listed the definitions of philosophy known to him. Seneca derives the word itself from 'love' and 'wisdom' and calls philosophy 'the love of wisdom'; he also describes it as 'love of right reason'; 'the study of virtue'; and the art of thinking aright, 'the study of mental correction' (*corrigende mentis*) (Lafleur, pp. 306–7, and Seneca, *Ep.* 89). Arnulf gathers another sheaf of definitions from the nature of philosophy *a parte rei*. Calcidius says that philosophy is 'the certain knowledge of both things seen and things unseen'. Gundissalinus and Isidore say that it is 'the certain knowledge of divine and human matters, conjoined with the study of right living' (Lafleur, p. 308). Isidore also offers the notion that philosophy is the art of arts and the science of sciences. Or philosophy may be said to be the study by which man grows closer to his Creator by the virtue proper to humanity (Lafleur, p. 309). Or philosophy is 'order benefitting the soul' (*ordo anime conveniens*), or 'man's self-knowledge', or 'the care, study and anxiety which relate to death', or 'the inquiry into nature and the knowledge of divine and human matters insofar as that is possible for man' (Lafleur, p. 310). And since sometimes 'philosophy' is used interchangeably with 'wisdom' or 'knowledge', the definitions of these terms too are relevant to the understanding of philosophy (Lafleur, p. 311).[12]

Something is also to be learned about the thirteenth-century notion of what philosophy is from an account of what it is not. One such *accessus* specifically excludes the mechanical and magical arts from philosophy. The mechanical arts, divided in the ancient way into weaving, arms-making, navigation, hunting, agriculture, medicine and theatre, are seen as positively opposed to philosophy because they 'teach the spirit to serve the flesh', which is the opposite of the purpose of philosophy. Magic is seen as beyond the pale of all other sciences, multifarious in its fivefold disciplines of divination, augury (*mathematica*), maleficent works, the casting of lots on the future, and illusion, a rogue study, neither liberal nor 'servile' (Lafleur, pp. 285–7).

Later authors were to continue the debate, and it was never to be possible to exclude the magical arts from philosophy altogether. Jean

Gerson, for example, wrote in 1402 that philosophers think it probable that demons exist, and faith tells us it is a matter of certainty.[13] Magic is real. The problem is not that it is a pseudo-science but that it stands in the way of truth by directing the mind to bodily, sensible and particular things.[14] It does so in a more dangerous way than the mechanical sciences, which are merely unworthy of study. Magic involves making pacts with demons, and that is a form of idolatry.[15] It is inclined to vulgar error, too, because its operations flout the laws of nature.[16] When we turn to magicians we break faith with God, growing impatient because he does not seem to hear our prayers or respond to our efforts to fast and go on pilgrimages.[17] While it was believed that magic works, its study and practice continued to obtrude on those of philosophy and theology alike. The same was true for astrology. Gerson wrote in 1419, acknowledging that the heavens are God's instrument of government, and their motions more than mere signs. Astrologers, he says, must remember that their art is theology's handmaid and then they will not fall into impious errors and sacrilegious superstitions.[18]

The concepts of theology and philosophy, and of the peripheral sciences, the liberal arts, the mechanical arts, even the magical arts, can all be seen as hierarchically ordered to the supreme purpose of knowing God. It was generally held in the thirteenth century that the mechanical arts operate at such a humble level that they are not worth the study of those who are capable of learning better things, and indeed they may distract the soul from aspiring higher. The magical arts and astrology have a built-in tendency to error, because they do not have their sights fixed on God alone (although they are effective enough in the mediaeval view). The liberal arts ought to be theology's true handmaids, teaching skills which enable the soul to do theology (*theologizare*) better. But philosophy herself is too close to theology for comfort. She can be seen as embracing all these other arts and sciences, and also some of the area proper to theology itself.

A first conclusion to be drawn from all this is that the thirteenth-century masters got no further than their predecessors in 'placing' philosophy incontrovertibly among the arts and sciences. Nor did they succeed in defining the exact scope of the discipline in a manner with which everyone could agree. Philosophy was not like grammar or logic, with familiar elementary or more advanced textbooks, and an established place in the syllabus. Nevertheless, in practice, it was the study of the *artes* which proved best able to accommodate the influx of new textbooks on philosophical subjects when the rest of Aristotle arrived in the West from the end of the twelfth century. That led, as we shall see, to inter-Faculty rivalry in the universities. But before we come to that story we must look at the development in the Middle Ages of a corresponding 'idea of theology'.

THE IDEA OF THEOLOGY AND THE CONFLICT OF INTERESTS

The term *theologia* was not normally used in Christian writers for what we should now call 'theology' until the thirteenth century. Until the twelfth century it was more usual to speak of 'the study of Holy Scripture'. Even Aquinas, late in the thirteenth century, speaks of *sacra doctrina* in the *Summa Theologiae* in preference to *theologia*. The notion of a discipline which amounted to the systematic study of the Christian faith by rational methods grew only slowly and uncertainly out of the study of the Bible, and by analogy with other sciences.

But the word *theologia* was familiar enough in a narrower and more restricted sense, which was known in the earlier Middle Ages from Boethius. Boethius defines *theologia* as a branch of philosophy, or *speculativa* (*De Trinitate*, II). The subject-matter of *physica*, natural science, is body and form taken together, studied in motion. That of mathematics is the investigation of pure form, as though that could be abstracted from matter and motion, but with the recognition that in reality it cannot. Theology deals with that which is wholly free of matter and motion, the divine Substance. This distinction, which Boethius borrows from Plato by way of more recent Platonist thought,[19] 'places' theology in relation to other human intellectual endeavour, but at the cost of limiting its scope from a Christian point of view. For Boethius, writing as a philosopher-Christian, the burning questions of the day were in any case still those of the debate of the first Christian centuries about the nature of God, his Trinity and his relation to his creation. Only in the *De Fide Catholica* does he go beyond these topics, confronting the difficulty that it is necessary to bring in the evidence of revelation which philosophers will not necessarily accept, if one is to explain the events of man's Fall, the Incarnation and the redemption of the world.

The centrality of revealed truth became the linch-pin of the mediaeval definition of *theologia*. One thirteenth-century author distinguishes between 'divine' and 'human' sciences, and explains that 'the divine is that which is handed down directly from God, such as theology' (Lafleur, p. 259). It was possible to contrast this Christian *theologia* with the Boethian usage (Lafleur, p. 323).

Arnulfus Provincialis explains that theology has its *causa* in man's fall into sin. Adam was created in the image and likeness of God, perfect in virtue and knowledge (*scientiae*), but he transgressed against the law of nature laid upon him, and his *oculus intellectualis*, the eye of understanding, was darkened and blinded and ceased to see truly. The damage was done not only to his soul, but also to his body. There is, however, a further *causa* in the unavoidable creaturely limitation of Adam. He was designed to strive to be more perfect, that is, to grow more like his Creator by acquiring virtue and knowledge; he ought to lift up his soul in contemplation of his Creator and find there his soul's happiness. This is described, says Arnulf, by the philosophers. (He cites Algazel in the *Metaphysics*.)

Arnulf argues that it is therefore appropriate and necessary for fallen humanity to study philosophy as a means to that growth towards perfection in virtue and knowledge which is necessary if they are to be saved from the consequences of the Fall. 'By the discipline of philosophy we are led to the knowledge of all being, to love and fear and reverence for the Creator of such marvellous creatures' (Lafleur, pp. 303–5).

Aquinas found it necessary to put first in his *Summa Theologiae* the question 'whether any further *doctrina* is required except philosophy' (*ST* I.q.1.a.1). His answer is that revelation (that is to say, Scriptural revelation) contains things which are necessary to salvation and which could never be found out by reason alone. He replies to two 'objections': first, that everything which can be treated by reason is dealt with by philosophy and man should not seek to know what is beyond the reach of his reason (Ecclesiasticus 3.22); secondly, that philosophy is concerned with all being, and therefore with all truth, which would seem to make theology a mere branch of philosophy, as Aristotle says (*Metaphysics* VI.1, 1026ª 19). The first, says Aquinas, does not take account of man's duty to accept by faith those things beyond reason which God reveals (Ecclesiasticus 25). The second forgets that the same subject-matter may be treated by different sciences. He stresses that the theology which pertains to sacred doctrine is of another order from that which is classically defined as a part of philosophy.

The same theme, that theology differs from philosophy in embracing the subject-matter of revelation, is to be found in Jean Gerson. At the turn of the fourteenth century, he conducted an experiment with Boethius' *Consolation of Philosophy*. He wrote a dialogue between 'Volucer' and 'Monicus', *On the Consolation of Theology*, in the same prosimetric form as Boethius. The question addressed is why philosophy alone is not enough to give true consolation. Volucer explains to Monicus that theology bears the same sort of relationship to philosophy as grace to nature, mistress to maid, understanding (*intelligentia*) to reasoning (*ratiocinatio*); it is appropriate that there should be order and *gradus* in the sciences, and theology proceeds in the most orderly and economical way (*recto breviatoque ordine procedet*) if she builds her inferences upon the foundation of philosophy. The text is therefore a useful indication of Gerson's view of the relationship between philosophy and theology. He develops the point in several ways. He sees philosophy as excluding matters which can be known only by revelation. God, he says, could see that human beings were making mistakes and that they could not arrive at 'necessary and saving truths' by means of philosophy. So he revealed the subject-matter of theology to them 'supernaturally' (*supernaturaliter*) (p. 189). The most significant addition, which he picks on at once, is the knowledge of the 'order' of divine judgement (p. 190). Within that framework of a providence which goes beyond anything Boethius describes in the *Consolatio Philosophiae* he sets his lengthy discussion of predestination and Christian hope. The philosophers of the gentiles, he explains, could see that God exists, but the mystery of the Incarnation can be grasped only if it is explicitly revealed (*explicite revelatum*), and it must be believed by faith. Grace is given only through the medium of the Mediator of God and men (*per medium Mediatoris Dei et hominum*). He merited grace sufficiently for all, but it has effect only in those who are incorporated in him by 'habitual faith', as in children, or the actual and habitual faith which shows itself in adults through perseverance in love.[20]

This development from a 'Boethian' to a mediaeval Christian notion of the scope of *theologia* had implications for the view that philosophy is the guide of life. Moral theology filled that need for Christians. There remained, nevertheless, the awkwardness of the common element of *speculativa*. In Boethian handling of the topics of *theologia*, as in the treatment of the same subjects (in their different ways) by classical philosophers, it was uncontroversial that all the aids to formal reasoning which grammar, logic and rhetoric could provide should be employed. Such aids were not less helpful in the Middle Ages. In fact they were more helpful, because there were major technical developments in these areas. But for some mediaeval scholars there arose the question whether reason could properly be used in this way in discussing matters of faith. On the whole, it was not an urgent problem in the earlier Middle Ages. The cognate question, the one which troubled Jerome, was more pressing then, and we find Christian scholars debating whether or not they ought to be reading and using secular literary authors or whether they risked being 'Ciceronian' rather than Christian if they did so. Even for Anselm, late in the eleventh century, faith and formal reasoning went comfortably hand in hand as faith sought understanding (*Proslogion*, 1). But from the eleventh century, with increasing student interest in the possibilities of using grammar and logic in particular, reasoning seemed sometimes to be challenging the faith. A little after 1215, William of Auxerre states the view that it is 'perverse' to try to prove articles of faith by human reason.[21] Faith cannot be established by proof; indeed, if it could be demonstrated by human reason alone it would have no merit.[22] He gives a list of heretics such as Arius and Sabellius,[23] who were deceived by their reason into error.[24]

The issue here was whether theological truths could or could not be established by philosophical methods, that is (as Gilbert Crispin and Peter Abelard took it), by appeal to human reason alone. If that were possible, then philosophy had a proper and even a necessary place in theological discourse. But at the same time, theology would be thrown open to all the visible disadvantages of philosophical debate, with no certainty that the outcome would conform with the orthodox teaching of the Church down the centuries. If – as conservative opinion always stoutly held – theological truths could not ultimately be so established, there remained the question as to how far philosophical arguments might still be useful as corroborative or supportive means of presenting truths of faith.

Augustine regarded the best of the philosophers as friends to the Christian cause, because by the light of reason they had understood, at least in principle, some of Christianity's fundamental truths. He says that Christians may therefore 'spoil the Egyptians' with a clear conscience, and carry off gold, silver and precious vessels as the Hebrews did when they left Egypt (*De Doct. Chr.* II.40.60). He did not advocate unselective plunder. He gives up a long stretch of *The City of God* (Book VIII) to a comparison of the schools of thought known to him, and concludes that the Platonists came closest to glimpsing Christian truth. But he sees no insuperable objection to the concept of a 'Christian philosophy' (*C. Jul.* IV.14.72).[25]

Augustine's successors were not all able to be as sanguine as he. The mediaeval fear was that philosophy might encroach upon theology or even take it over, if allowed free reign. From at least the late twelfth century we find complaints being voiced that the disciplines are in disorder, and in particular that philosophy is overflowing its proper bounds and contaminating other subjects. Stephen of Tournai wrote to the Pope in the last decade of the twelfth century to say that the very garments of philosophy are torn and disordered; she is no longer consulted as she used to be, and she is therefore no longer able to console.[26] More commonly the complaint runs the other way. A thirteenth-century Dominican says that scholars are behaving like barbarians, corrupting theology by introducing metaphysics even into the study of Holy Scripture.[27]

That anxiety is expressed again and again (though philosophy is not always a pejorative term).[28] In the late twelfth century, a satirical attack on the 'four Labyrinths' of France (Gilbert of Poitiers, Peter Abelard, Peter of Poitiers, Peter Lombard) asks what is the place of the study of the liberal arts, secular authors and especially philosophers, and works its way through the teaching of named philosophers, explaining what is unacceptable in each. Plato, for example, believes that the stars are gods; Aristotle's argumentation is full of trickery.[29] Soon afterwards Alan of Lille criticises a tendency to apply terms taken from natural science to the study of theology, with the result that those scarcely capable of understanding common theatre presume to be able to understand the disputations of angels.[30] Theologians and Masters of Arts trod upon one another's toes as they disputed such matters as the special usage of nouns and verbs in Holy Scripture. It need hardly be said that these anxieties would not have arisen had there not been unavoidable areas of overlap and the discovery of rich possibilities in one another's areas.

Philosophical study had an unsettling effect because it was recognised that it was not necessarily bent on securing the truth. We find the contrast drawn between 'speaking in a philosophical way' and 'speaking theologically and according to the truth'.[31] Philosophy was allowed to explore for curiosity's sake, and without an obligation to produce solutions harmonious with Christian truth.[32] Roger Bacon in the thirteenth century distinguishes between the vices of philosophy, notably that of curiosity for its own sake, and a use of philosophy in support of theological study.[33] He can envisage philosophy faithfully serving her mistress, investigating causes of error so that truth may become plain, and indeed herself supporting and securing truth and driving out error. But this was optimistic, and it was not what most theologians expected to be the result of letting philosophical study go its own way.

There were many points at which particular philosophical teachings unavoidably conflicted directly with Christian faith: on transmigration of souls, for example, or on the eternity of the created world. Does God have power to make a body present in two places at once? Do angels 'know' things whose futurity is contingent? Can the heavens ever stop moving of themselves? Does the agent intellect remain in the soul when it is separated from the body? All these questions occur in the *Quodlibets* or miscellaneous questions of Giles of Rome (printed Louvain, 1546). Between about 1268 and 1274 Giles published a list of *Errores Philosophorum*[34] in which he takes one by one, Aristotle, Averroes, Avicenna and Maimonides, and sets out the key points at which their opinions are incompatible with Christian truth. Aristotle, for example, thought that all change is preceded by motion (I.1), that time had no beginning (I.2), that the world is eternal (I.3), the heavens ungenerated and incorruptible (I.4); he denies the resurrection of the dead (I.9). Averroes reasserts his errors, but with still more force. The world, he says, had no beginning; God has no providential care for individual beings; there is no Trinity in God; the Intellect is numerically one in all beings (IV.6–10). Avicenna, too, is seen as repeating Aristotle's errors and making them more enormous. He contends that no changing thing can proceed directly from an unchanging God (VI.4); God cannot know the individual natures of our descriptions of singular things (VI.13); God's attributes apply only by remotion and do not denote anything positive in him (VI.14); intelligences cannot be evil (VI.12). Maimonides erred in believing that the Word and the Spirit of God are not Persons, but expressions of God's presence only (XII.4); that prophets are self-made (XII.7). It is this sort of conflict between philosophical speculation and Christian truth which is reflected in the 219 Articles condemned at Paris in 1277.[35]

Most importantly, there were respects in which Christians held themselves to have not only the whole truth, where philosophers had only a part of it, but also that truth which is necessary to salvation. Philosophers might come close in their thinking on the nature of God and his Word, on the illumination of the understanding, even at points on creation's relationship to the Godhead; but they did not share the doctrine of Incarnation or the heritage of revealed historical evidences (cf. Augustine, *De Trinitate* IV.16.21 and *De Vera Religione* 7.13).

In the face of the practical and unavoidable reality of conflict between what 'the philosophers' say and what the Church teaches, several increasingly familiar *topoi* make their appearance. We meet in later forms the disquiet already referred to, which Jerome voiced when he had an uncomfortable vision of himself as Ciceronianus, not Christianus.[36] Stephen of Tournai, for instance, writing in the last decade of the twelfth century, says that the Christian should not waste his time *in figmentis poeticis*, or on grammar, rhetoric, law, medicine, geometry or *in perplexionibus Aristotelis*. His point is that although the liberal arts are helpful in understanding the Scriptures, taken in their own right readings of 'the literature of the gentiles' (*litterarum gentilium*) do not illuminate but darken the mind.[37] They are dangerously seductive but empty. Prepositinus, Chancellor of Paris from 1206 to 1210, makes a similar point. Philosophy and dialectic, he says, see with the eye of 'vain wisdom' (*vana sapientia*); they behold clouds and vanity. Philosophy is a sterile chattering (*infecunda loquacitas*), a useless subtlety and a subtle uselessness. If we approach the study of Holy Scripture 'philosophically' (*philosophice*), we shall displease God.[38]

The double commonplace of 'despoiling the Egyptians' and the theme of the captured handmaid are also frequent. The notion that the Greek philosophers stole their wisdom from the Hebrews, but distorted the truths they had learned, derives from Clement of Alexandria (*Stromateis* I.81.4). Augustine transmitted the belief to the mediaeval West, though with a number of reservations about the dating (*De Doctrina Christiana* II.43; *De Civitate Dei* VIII.ii). In his letter of 1228 to the Masters of Theology at Paris, Gregory IX opens with a reference to the theme, in the confidence that his meaning will be understood at once. 'Vessels of gold and silver are to be received by the Hebrews from the Egyptians, so that they might grow rich, not so that they should become their slaves in payment' (cf. Exodus 11).[39] He extends the metaphor to include the theme of the captured handmaid (cf. Deuteronomy 21.10ff.). This too had a long earlier history. Philo of Alexandria explores the implications of the idea that the arts are properly the handmaids of the study of Scripture in his discussion of Hagar.[40] The principle is to be found widely in mediaeval writers, Peter Damian,[41] Rupert of Deutz,[42] Stephen of Tournai and Bonaventure,[43] to take a few instances. The argument is that, as handmaids, secular studies have a useful task to perform, but it is essentially one of service. They must always be subordinate to their mistress, Theology, and their beauty and seductiveness must not be allowed to captivate the student to the point where he gives them first place in his affections. It is an indication of their powers of attraction that the lesson needed to be repeated so frequently.

2

PHILOSOPHICAL SOURCES

SCHOOLS AND SCHOLARS

The assimilation of the philosophical source-materials at which we shall be looking in a moment depended in the earlier Middle Ages upon the individual enterprise of a few scholars. Bede is outstanding among the generations which salvaged ancient learning from the wreck of the Roman Empire. In the Carolingian period, Charlemagne's insistence that cathedrals should run schools for the clergy meant that an institutional framework came into being outside the monasteries, in which there could be some systematic teaching of the basics of the liberal arts and the study of Scripture and the Fathers. Carolingian scholars, some working largely as private scholars as Eriugena did, some within the schools (Remigius of Auxerre) made an enormous contribution to the slow work of opening up the possibilities of ancient scholarship to a world from which its preoccupations had become largely remote. The same pattern of individual and school-based work, proceeding more or less haphazardly, continues until the late eleventh century. Then the schools began to multiply, especially at first in northern France, and to attract young men of talent and ambition. In the course of the twelfth century sufficient foundations were laid for the schools to begin to grow into universities. By the end of the fifteenth century Europe had more than seventy universities, disseminating knowledge internationally.

In all teaching institutions from Carolingian times at least, the staple method of teaching was the 'reading' of a text with the students. The master would normally begin with an introduction or *accessus* in which he explained who the author was, what was his purpose in writing, what branch of philosophy the book belonged to, and what was to be gained from studying it.[1] In time, the comments on the text itself evolved from what were often mere notes on the grammatical structure or synonyms for difficult words, to remarks on difficult points in the content. By the early twelfth century such remarks could be lengthy, and contain cross-references to other texts or to the opinions of rival masters. Peter Abelard's lectures on the dialectical set books reveal a lively exchange of this sort in the Paris of his day. Out of these lengthening critical comments grew 'questions'. By the middle of the twelfth century, Simon of Tournai and others were setting aside time in the afternoon in which points raised in the lectures which were too complex to be handled in the cursory reading could be considered at leisure. These occasions became 'disputations', when master and pupils would debate issues both of long-standing and of current topicality. The disputation proved a convenient vehicle for the newly qualified master to prove himself and win pupils; on special occasions it provided opportunities for what in the later Middle Ages was clearly sometimes almost a theatrical display of erudition and quick-wittedness; the *theses*, or subjects for debate, would be posted in advance and the disputation would attract not only a university audience but also a large crowd of townspeople who came to see a good fight. Luther's posting of the Ninety-Five Theses on the church door at Wittenberg in 1517 was just such a challenge.

Although the basic method of 'teaching a text' was common to Arts Faculties and Faculties of Theology alike, as was the use of the disputation to deal with questions, the standing of the texts of classical philosophy was not quite the same in all university departments. They might be brought in as 'authorities' in an argument in theology; but only in the Arts Faculties were they studied as set books. Even here there was some degree of variation. Paris was always important for logic, and even in the twelfth century it had an outstanding reputation for the study of the *artes*. From the middle of the thirteenth century Aristotle's *libri naturales* formed a standard part of the syllabus, especially in Paris. But it is at Oxford in the fourteenth century that we find mathematics and natural science especially flourishing. It is something of a paradox that although it was the Arts Faculties which claimed the philosophical texts as their special province for study, it was often in theology that the most inventive and searching use was made of them, as senior scholars who had been through the arts courses made application of philosophical principles to the supremely testing problems which arose in theology.

The coming of Aristotle's works on natural science and metaphysics caused a crisis in thirteenth-century Paris. In 1210 the teaching of these works was banned at the provincial synod of Sens, under the presidency of the archbishop, Peter of Corbeil, who had himself been a Master of Theology and Canon Law at Paris in the 1190s.[2] At the same time, two contemporary scholars were anathematised. The destruction of the books of Amaury of Bène and David of Dinant was so successful in eradicating their teaching that it is now difficult to reconstruct it exactly.[3] The coupling of the problem posed by these two *heretici* and that presented by Aristotle is both instructive and misleading. It shows us that the study of Aristotle was felt to pose a threat to orthodoxy. But it obscures the character of the study itself, and the novelty of the danger it presented.

There seems little doubt that the campaign to bring about the ban was led by the Faculty of Theology at Paris.[4] The underlying rivalry between the Masters of Arts and the Masters of Theology could not have shown itself in quite this way before the organisation of the university had developed sufficiently for the Faculties to emerge. In the twelfth century we find some indications that Masters lecturing on logic, for instance, were tending to avoid using theological examples, tempting though some questions were to a logician.[5] This can be put down to the sense expressed in connection with Peter Abelard by an outraged St Bernard and others, that it was a serious matter to set oneself up as a theologian; it required lengthy study and humility on the part of a scholar. Abelard had offended by moving from arts to theology over-night and claiming that he could do as well as any professional. But alongside this sense of a proper decency, and the need for respect for the supreme study of the human intellect, must be set the practical consid-eration that while everyone studied arts, theology was, already in the twelfth century, a higher study to which comparatively few went on when they had finished the arts course.[6] The theologians of Paris in 1210 were alarmed to see the Masters of Arts stalking their territory, Aristotle in hand, and not merely the now fairly familiar volumes of the logic, but books on subjects germane to the study of the very Being of God, the creation of the world and the nature of man, which went far beyond anything which had been available in the twelfth century. David of Dinant himself seems to have been both one of the first to study the newly arrived texts, and a prime example of a scholar whose grasp on orthodoxy had gone askew under their influence.[7] The purpose of the ban of 1210 was to stop this dangerous trend at its source, by preventing the teaching of the new 'scientific' Aristotle in the Arts Faculty.

The anxiety of the Paris theologians was sufficiently infectious for Robert Courson to repeat and enlarge it in 1215, acting as papal legate. His is a text which mixes the purposes of stature, privilege and ban. It lays down the difference of status between Masters of Arts and theo-logians in terms of their respective ages and minimum qualifications. A Master of Arts is to be at least twenty-one years of age and to have six years' study in the *artes* behind him. No one may lecture in theology before he is thirty-five and he must have at least eight years' study, five of them in theology.[8] There is a list of the works of Aristotle which may be covered in arts lectures. Those *de metafisica et de naturali philosophia* are banned, together with *summae* of their contents. The ban got into the contemporary press. Several chroniclers mention it, and in connection with the fear that the study of the new Aristotle on natural science and metaphysics 'was giving occasion for subtle heretical opinions'.[9]

It need hardly be said that the bans of 1210 and 1215 were ineffective. The study of Aristotle continued, even if only informally and privately within the university, and in the course of the following decade or so it became possible to take stock rather more calmly of its implications, and to see beyond the local rivalry engendered by the readiness of jumped-up Masters of Arts to invade the territory of the theologians with their new knowledge. In July 1228 Gregory IX wrote a moderate and cautiously worded warning to the scholars of Paris, wrapped up in silk.

This was followed a year or two later by the *Parens Scientiarum* of 1231. Taken together, the two texts constitute, if not a *volte-face*, certainly a substantial shift of ground on the subject of the condemned works of Aristotle. In his initial letter Gregory talks in general terms about the relationship between theology and philosophy. He begins with a classic description of the right way to 'spoil the Egyptians' (Exodus 11.7). *Theologicus intellectus* ought to be the dominant partner, like a man in his relations with the handmaid captured from an enemy. There ought to be no *commixtio* of philosophy and theology. Theology should proceed according to approved tradition. When faith is balanced on a structure of reasoning it is made vain and unprofitable, for faith has no merit if it depends on human reason. Gregory does not name Aristotle here or refer directly to the condemnations of 1210 and 1215.[10] *Parens Scientiarum* is more explicit. Gregory provides for the use of the *libri naturales* when they have been purged of errors by a committee set up by him, but restricts them to the Faculty of Arts.[11] To the members of his committee, William Archdeacon of Beauvais and two Canons of Rheims, he writes with instructions to look for anything in the books which is *virulens* 'or otherwise vicious', 'which can detract from the purity of the faith'.[12] He accepts that there is useful as well as dangerous matter in the new Aristotle, and his concern is simply to prevent stumbling-blocks being put in the way of the faithful.[13]

This would seem to be an exercise in 'damage limitation'. It had become clear that the study of Aristotle's *libri naturales* was not going to be stopped by ban. The University of Toulouse, newly founded and touting for custom, had sent a circular to other universities in 1229 promising that 'the books on natural science which were banned at Paris, can be heard there by those who wish to gaze into the heart of nature's secrets'.[14] In any case, the ideas the books contained were already being disseminated and were infiltrating the very fabric of theological discourse. Gregory will have known that his attempt to have them purged must be unsuccessful, because the objectionable matter could not now be finally got rid of. In any case, his committee never finished its work because William of Beauvais died soon after being appointed.

Within two decades a pattern was established. On the one hand, the books which had caused disquiet had a settled place in the syllabus of the Faculty of Arts. At Paris, the regulations of 1255 list the *Physics*, the *Metaphysics*, the *De Animalibus*, the *De Celo et Mundo*, parts of the *Meteorology*, the *De Anima*, the *De Generatione*, the *De Sensu et Sensato*, the *De Sompno et Vigilia*, the *De Plantis*, the *De Memoria et Reminiscentia*, the *De Differentia Spiritus et Animae*, *De Morte et Vita*, *De Causis* – among them, of course, more than pure Aristotle.[15] Lecturers are given a minimum time to cover each, but may take longer. On the other hand, signs of strain in the system are apparent in the condemnation of errors at Paris in 1241, by the Masters of Theology and Odo, Chancellor of Paris.[16] Condemnations and agitation occurred in the 1260s and 1270s, over Averroes as well as Aristotle.[17] A Statute of the Faculty of Arts at Paris for 1272 says that Masters of Arts must not deal with theological questions, and that where they treat questions which touch on the faith as well as on philosophy they must never determine the matter in a manner which goes against orthodoxy. Ockham is careful to explain that when he gives an opinion which contradicts something Scripture says, or the *determinatio et doctrina* of the Roman Church, or the *sententia* of doctors approved by the Church, he speaks not as one asserting such a view, but merely 'in the person' of one who does.[18] The Paris Faculty of Arts in 1339 promulgated a decree against those who were teaching novel doctrines of William of Ockham, before there had been time to assess them to make sure they contained nothing damaging to the faith. It censures those who make such a tumult by heckling in the *disputatio* that the truth of the conclusion being arrived at becomes obscured, and those who go to the disputations to listen and learn are not able to get any benefit from them. A statute of 1340 follows this up by asserting that every Master is duty bound to do his best to avoid errors and to keep clear of lines of argument which may lead to errors. Some members of the Faculty of Arts are blamed for indulging in pernicious subtleties, not only in philosophy, but even in their comments on theological points and points of Scripture.[19] In the mid-fourteenth century, Buridan refers to the oath taken in the previous century by those incepting in arts, that they will not dispute theological questions, and if they touch on such matters by chance, will always determine in favour of the orthodox teaching of the Church.

THE CLASSICAL SOURCES OF MEDIAEVAL PHILOSOPHY

The influence of Greek and Roman philosophical texts upon the Christian theology of the Middle Ages was both direct and indirect. In many cases the books were available to be read for themselves. But there were also layers upon layers of intermediate influence. Macrobius, for example, commented upon Cicero's *Dream of Scipio* and provided his mediaeval readers with material on Pythagorean mathematics, Platonic cosmology and much else in the process. Christian patristic authors were themselves a means by which classical philosophical ideas were diffused in the mediaeval West: most notably Augustine, but also Origen, Jerome and Gregory the Great, with Ambrose of Milan giving a glimpse of the Cappadocian Fathers, and through them additional elements of the background of Greek thought. And there is, of course, the possibility that sometimes a scholar hit on a problem or its solution for himself and then barricaded his position with authorities.

The most significant barrier to the direct transmission, of the Greek texts in particular, was the problem of language. In Augustine's day it was a matter of mild embarrassment to an educated Latin-speaker to be unable to read Greek fluently. By the time of Gregory the Great (c.540–604) the language-barrier was dividing the Empire as clearly as was the political situation. Bede knew only a few words of Greek. John Scotus Eriugena (c.810–77) was almost unique in Carolingian times in the mastery he achieved of a language which by now was likely to have to be learned in the West from books and not from native speakers. It was sufficiently clear to Boethius that Greek works were becoming inaccessible to Latin-speakers, indeed that the legacy of the Greek world was at risk, for him to put in hand the project of translating the whole of Plato and Aristotle. He had completed only a small part of it before his death. It is apparent that he was right, for the West had to make do with what he had provided until the twelfth century, when translation from the Arabic renderings of Aristotle, and to a lesser extent direct from the Greek again, made parts of ancient Greek thought more fully accessible.

It is not too much to say that the whole history of Western thought was shaped until then by the chance which gave it small Aristotle and almost no Plato.

Cassiodorus, Boethius' contemporary, also saw that Greek learning was in danger of being lost to the West, but his plan was to make encyclopaedic summaries of the essentials of the disciplines for use in teaching. His *Institutiones* served their purpose, and became a model for Isidore in his *Etymologiae* and for the Carolingian encyclopaedists later. But in the nature of things they could do little to sustain or further serious philosophical enquiry.

The Greek philosophical tradition remained, then, at a linguistic disadvantage for many centuries after the fall of the Roman Empire. It was in any case limited in its influence throughout the Middle Ages where it had to be read in Latin, because the Latin language remained a less happy vehicle for abstract speculation than Greek (despite Cicero's efforts to stretch and adapt it, and Boethius' attempts to take his achievements further). In the high Middle Ages Latin became a technically exact instrument for the logician's and metaphysician's purposes, but it never matched ancient Greek in its capacity for subtlety of expression. To this intrinsic disadvantage of Latin must be added the awkwardness and often the inaccuracy of translations made in an earnest effort to render word for word and by scholars whose Greek was almost never as fluent as their Latin, or who were (in the twelfth and thirteenth centuries) sometimes working from a rendering into Arabic and not directly from the Greek.

Roger Bacon, who was a passionate advocate of the study of languages, believed that the comparative poverty of Latin philosophy in the ancient world was due to a failure to translate all the work of the Greeks into Latin. He thought that the works of Plato had been generally known to the Romans, but not those of Aristotle, because he had been Plato's opponent. He praises Augustine for having (as he believed) translated the *Categories* (for his son), and mentions that Boethius had translated some of Aristotle's logic (*Opus Maius* I.xiii).

It is worth pausing for a moment over Bacon's account of the transmission of ancient philosophical learning (although Bacon is something of an eccentric), because it gives us an insight into the picture thirteenth-century scholars themselves had of what had happened and how their sources had reached them. Bacon thinks it important to make the link between Christian history and the history of philosophy. That can be shown from Aristotle, Cicero and Augustine (*Opus Maius* II.vi). He used the Old Testament patriarchs as instructors. Josephus tells us that Noah and his sons taught philosophy to the Chaldeans and that Abraham taught the Egyptians. Even Aristotle admits that philosophy began with the patriarchs (*Opus Maius* II.ix). Ancient philosophy developed from that point in parallel with Hebrew learning (*Opus Maius* II.ix–x). Bacon knew the names and 'schools' of Greek thinkers from Thales of Miletus, through the Pythagoreans to Socrates, Plato and Aristotle. He can name Anaximander, Anaximenes, Anaxagoras and Archelaus on the way. (He does not accept that Plato studied under Jeremiah the Prophet while he was in Egypt, as some believe he did, because the chronology will not fit (*Opus Maius* II.xi–xii)). He sees Aristotle as the greatest and last of this line, a philosopher who almost succeeded in bringing philosophy back to the perfection in which it had been given to the patriarchs of old. But he made mistakes, and it is still possible to improve on what he said (*Opus Maius* II.xiii). Thus, while regarding the philosophical tradition as God-given and parallel to the Christian, Bacon feels free to criticise and amend the work of the philosophers. It was necessary to justify doing so, for this heritage of ancient philosophical learning did not pass easily into the Christian tradition. This was so, Bacon explains, because the pagans persecuted the Christians at first, and the Church found herself confronted by philosophers who were also enemies. Moreover, these hostile philosophers seemed to Christian eyes, he says, to be intellectually and morally tainted by the study of magical arts. This suspicion has lingered, he comments, although it is no longer justified. It meant that Christians were not at ease in using the philosophers and had to wait for most of Aristotle until Moslem scholars brought his work to light and their work began to find its way to the Christian West, he explains (*Opus Maius* II.xiii and I.xiv–v).

Plato, Platonism

Early Christian thought was permeated by a diffuse Platonism. Platonism was itself a living and creative philosophical tradition during the first Christian centuries, and coincidences of thinking were plain to Christian readers. Augustine, who had never, as far as we know, gone to the trouble of making any special study of Cicero's translation of part of Plato's *Timaeus*, or to seek out Calcidius' fourth-century commentary on it, or to look for the other dialogues he could have found at Carthage or Rome, was captivated when an acquaintance showed him Marius Victorinus' recent renderings of Plotinus and Porphyry. He read there, he says, of the Word of God, who was in the beginning with God, and by

24

whom all things were made (*Confessions* VII.ix). This and much more showed him hints of a truth beyond sense-perception and began to satisfy at last the intellectual and spiritual hunger which had kept him searching for a decade and more for a philosophical and religious system which would not fail him (*Confessions* VII.xx). Thus was the ground laid for his conversion to a Christianity which was for Augustine always to be in sympathy with much Platonist teaching. It was Platonism, for example, which taught him the principle that sin and evil create darkness in the mind, and gave him some understanding of an omnipresent, unchanging God (*Confessions* VII.xx). There was much that Platonism could not do for him, as he explains. He discovered in Scripture truths beyond the understanding of the philosophers (*Confessions* VII.xxi). But there was a comforting amount of common ground for Augustine, and others before him who had wanted to make use of the most sophisticated philosophical works of their time in trying to understand express Christian truth. Platonism encouraged an emphasis on the spiritual and aspiring, where the clear air of the knowledge of God was attained by self-denial, subjugation of the flesh and the cultivation of intellectual purity, and a man's soul could rise above his baser nature. Christ could be seen as the highest Reason, God's Wisdom. It seemed to Augustine not only an appropriate but a natural move to go into 'philosophical retirement' at Cassiciacum for a time after his conversion, to discuss with friends such questions as the nature of the happy life (*De Beata Vita*) and the order of the universe (*De Ordine*).

It was in practice largely through Augustine's writings that much of Platonism's system of thought came to enter so fully and deeply into the Western Christian tradition. But the Pseudo-Dionysian tradition also played a part. In the fifth century Proclus wrote an *Elements of Theology* which was to prove controversial among contemporaries.[20] It provoked among other writings a series of works by an author who has become known as Ps.-Dionysius the Areopagite, in which the hierarchy of the universe under God is worked out in some detail, as an ascent towards union with God is set before man as his goal. Because these were held to be the writings of the Dionysius who was converted by St Paul they carried an almost apostolic authority in the centuries which followed, and through Ps.-Dionysius Proclus had a considerable influence in both Western and Eastern Christendom in the Middle Ages. The *Elements of Theology* itself was used by Michael Psellus in eleventh-century Byzantium, but in the West it did not become available in Latin until William of Moerbeke made his translation in 1268.

25

Plato's *Timaeus*, with Chalcidius' commentary, was in circulation in Latin in the West well before any other work of Plato was widely available. It was of particular interest in the twelfth century because it deals with creation, and challenges orthodox Christian teaching both in what it says about the question of creation *ex nihilo* and in its treatment of the *anima mundi*. Peter Abelard attempts to explain the difference of usage between Christian and 'philosopher' which makes it possible for 'the philosophers' to speak of a 'begetting of the world' (*genitura mundi*) and of God as *Genitor universitatis*, without meaning any more than that the world is 'from' (*ab*) God; while for the Christian 'begetting' is restricted to the relationship of Father to Son in the Trinity (*CCCM* XII, p. 82). Thierry of Chartres writes on the six days of creation with a sideways eye on Chalcidius (TC, pp. 555ff). Gilbert of Poitiers has Plato's ideas about the first matter in the forefront of his mind in writing about the way natural science studies matter and form (on Boethius' *De Trinitate*, GP, p. 80).

In the later twelfth century Henricus Aristippus translated the *Phaedo* and the *Meno*. But for the most part Plato's writings remained inaccessible to the mediaeval West. We find William of Auvergne speculating on what Plato himself might have said on a particular point,[21] and Guy of Rimini in the fourteenth century able only to speak of Aristotle's criticisms of Plato, without being in a position to say how Plato might have answered for himself.[22] It remained the case that the profound influence exercised by Plato upon mediaeval thought found its way for the most part indirectly through the works of later Platonists, and the Christian Fathers who had made use of their thought.

Aristotle

With Aristotle, the story is very different. First a portion of his logic, and then almost the entire corpus, were successively made available to mediaeval scholars in Latin translations.

By the end of the third century AD the six books of Aristotle's logic, later known as the *Organon*,[23] with commentaries by the third-century Porphyry, were the standard textbooks from which logic was taught. Porphyry had an influence here in his own right, which is to be seen in Ammonius (c.440–c.520), in Philoponus and Simplicius, who were Boethius' contemporaries, and in Boethius himself. Apuleius' *Periher-meneias* of the second century was also in use, and remained accessible to the early mediaeval West. But the core of the logical literature which was to form the basis of the early mediaeval course was Aristotelian.

Because of the temporary loss of all but Boethius' translations of the *Categories* and the *De Interpretatione* it was a limited Aristotelian logic that he transmitted to the early Middle Ages; but it was supplemented by his own commentaries on these books and on Porphyry's *Isagoge*, and by his monographs on cognate subjects. A conspicuous gap was a textbook on *Topics*. In default of Aristotle, that was filled for mediaeval scholars by Cicero's *Topica* (which indeed owes something to Aristotle); and by Boethius' *De Differentiis Topicis*, an attempt to reconcile the conflicting schools of thought of the ancient world on the subject. Cicero's *Topica* spawned another useful treatise. He comments (VI.28) that there are kinds of definition which he does not propose to treat; Marius Victorinus took up the challenge in his *De Definitione* and tried to complete the list. The *Decem Categoriae*, which was believed to be by Augustine, and Augustine's elementary *Dialectica* were also used, with outline summaries by the encyclopaedists. With the aid of these works the student could learn to classify and define, to construct propositions and basic syllogisms. He could get a glimpse of the possibilities of fallacies. He would be led into speculation on a number of issues of profound philosophical importance beyond logic: the nature of language; meaning; reference; the problem of future contingents. There was ample material for serious philosophical work here, although we have to wait until the eleventh century before more than the occasional exceptional individual seems to have made much of it.

This limited and contaminated Aristotelian logic was transformed in the twelfth century by the arrival of translations of the remaining books of the corpus of Aristotelian logic. The translations Boethius had made of the *Prior Analytics*, the *Topics* and the *Sophistici Elenchi* were recovered about 1120. James of Venice and an unknown Johannes made translations of the *Posterior Analytics*, although this last of Aristotle's logical works to come upon the mediaeval scene struck contemporaries as rebarbatively difficult, and it was not much exploited until the end of the century and the beginning of the next. Most attractive of all was the *Sophistici Elenchi*, with its delightful sophistical puzzles and its capacity to help in the resolution of a number of difficulties in the text of Scripture where one passage seemed to contradict another. Peter the Chanter made comprehensive use of it for this purpose in his *De Tropis Loquendi* at the end of the century.

Some of the *libri naturales* were turned into Latin in the twelfth century too. James of Venice translated the *Physics*, the *De Anima*, the beginning of the *Metaphysics* and five of the treatises known to later scholars as the *parva naturalia*. Henricus Aristippus translated Book IV of the *Meteorologica* before his death in 1162 and Gerard of Cremona made a version of the first three books afterwards from the Greek. Also from the Greek in the twelfth century were made Latin texts of the *De Generatione et Corruptione*, the *De Sensu*, the *De Somno* and others, also unattributable, of more of the *Metaphysics* (up to Book X, James of Venice having stopped in the fourth book) and part of the *Nicomachean Ethics*. Working this time from the Arabic, Gerard of Cremona produced texts of *Meteorologica* 1–3, the *Physics*, the *De Caelo* and the *De Generatione et Corruptione*. It would be hard to overstate the importance of contact with Arabic scholars, for the Arabs had long had a complete Aristotle and had themselves been writing both on Aristotle and upon the philosophical and scientific subjects he treats for generations. Those pioneering Christian scholars who went to Moslem Spain and elsewhere[24] in search of Greek philosophical literature in the twelfth century came back with more than they bargained for by way not only of texts but also of Arabic learning itself. Among the baggage, admittedly, was a good deal of Pseudo-Aristotle: *De Plantis* (in fact by Nicholas Damascenus and from the first century AD); Costa ben Luca's *De differentia Spiritus et Anima*; above all, the *De Causis*, which was Proclus' *Elements of Theology* in an Arabic paraphrase. Works of Arabic scholars such as Al-Kindi Algazel, Al-Farabi, Avencebrol[25] and Avicenna were available in Latin translations before the end of the twelfth century, and all these taught much that was Aristotelian.

Nevertheless, relatively little use was made in the twelfth century of any but the logical works of Aristotle. The necessary sub-structure of interest in the problems raised by the remainder was not yet sufficiently fully developed. They did not catch on among academics. They were not widely lectured upon in the schools. An exception such as Robert Grosseteste worked as a scholar with a private interest, finding his own way[26] across unfamiliar ground. There were a few more steps to be taken in making the full Aristotle available before it settled into its late mediaeval place as an indispensable tool of philosophical and theological enquiry. By 1220 Michael Scot had translated the three treatises of the *De Animalibus* and the commentaries of Averroes. The whole of the *Ethics* was also translated in the early thirteenth century, but Book I was circulated alone and was used without the remainder.[27] William of Moerbeke provided translations of what was missing otherwise and fresh translations of most of the new Aristotle. The logic and the natural science of Aristotle came to constitute two standard collections; William of Moerbeke's versions were used for the scientific texts and Boethius and James of Venice remained current for the logic.[28]

The Arabic philosophers who helped to transmit Aristotle to the mediaeval West had themselves had questions of theological compatibility to resolve. For Avicebron and Maimonides, who were Jews, the matter was even more complex. But their respect for Aristotle was very great, and in some measure they are all interpreters and explainers of Greek philosophical thought as well as Islamic scholars in their own right. The chief of these Arabic 'interpreters' of Aristotle in Western use was perhaps Averroes. Certainly his became a name to be bandied about in controversy when it seemed that philosophy was getting out of hand and forgetting to be a handmaid of theology. Avicenna's *Metaphysics* was also of particular importance because it could be set beside that of Aristotle. Avicenna, like other Arabs, took it for granted that the *De Causis* was Aristotle's, and also the 'Theology of Aristotle', drawn from Plotinus' *Enneads*, but circulating in the Middle Ages as Aristotle's work. Avicenna was therefore writing about a Platonised Aristotle, and in fact he has difficulty with the Platonic elements and tends to support Aristotle when he criticises Plato. But Avicenna is himself not uncritical of Aristotle and was prepared to put forward alternative and modified hypotheses.

A new series of translations of Aristotle and commentaries on his works began in the fifteenth century, but they belong to the story of the Renaissance.

The Stoics

By the end of the third century AD the works of Plato and Aristotle had become to some degree classics, and the later philosophical schools lost ground. Among them, Stoicism continued to have an influence of some significance in the West through the work of Seneca and also through Cicero. Seneca's *Epistulae Morales* and his *Moral Essays* cover such subjects as philosophy and friendship, philosophy as the guide of life, the true joy which comes from philosophy, the seclusion in which the philosopher should seem to live, the pursuit of moderation, how it is unworthy of a philosopher to quibble, how the philosopher should live in such a way that others are drawn to philosophy too, the value of self-control, and the seeking of the true good by reason. Seneca gives practical advice on becoming a philosopher by patient study, not attempting too much at once. He writes on tranquility of mind, and on subjects which engaged Augustine too in his retirement at Cassiciacum after his baptism: the blessed life, providence, and the need to have leisure for reflection.

Stoicism, perhaps more fully than any other ancient philosophical tradition, set out in a practical way the manner in which one might make philosophy the guide of life and grow in virtue as a result. Stoic thinking here was of a piece with Stoic physics: every being is seen as directed by a primary impulse towards its own preservation. For man that end is attained by systematically living in harmony with the natural world, by the light of a reason which sees man as a rational part of a rational whole. To live in that way is man's supreme good. There was nothing substantially at variance here with a Christian view of man's place in a universe ordered by providence, although the Stoic vision could be seen to fall short of the Christian one.

The Stoic material on natural science, especially Seneca's *Naturales Quaestiones*, furnished the West with its main source-material in this area until the arrival of Aristotle's *libri naturales* at the end of the twelfth century. (Though one should also include Pliny's *Natural History* here.)

A piece of Ps.-Seneca was also of some importance. The *De Copia Verborum* or *Sententie*, which is in fact the work of Publilius Syrus, circulated as a letter sent by Seneca to St Paul to improve his Latin, and was thus an established part of the Christian tradition and a ground for accepting Seneca, if not among Christian authors, at least as a warm sympathiser.

Cicero

Cicero was a significant source of knowledge of ancient philosophy for the mediaeval Latin West; to a degree his philosophical attainments do not perhaps merit in their own right. Cicero took up the writing of philosophy seriously when he was debarred from public life in 44 BC. He was obliged to look for comfort in philosophy, as Boethius was later to find it helpful to do in even more painful political circumstances. He wrote on aspects of the good life, and his books *On Friendship*, *On Old Age* and *On Duty* were to become staples of mediaeval libraries; they and the *Tusculan Disputations* coincided at many points with Christian ethics, and although they did not envisage the *beata vita* of the life to come in a Christian way, they could be regarded as improving reading for monks as well as worth academic study.

Cicero translated part of Plato's *Timaeus* and in *The Dream of Scipio* he ventured into cosmology as a means of giving an altogether larger perspective to his reflections on politics. He explored the arguments then current about the nature of the gods, ranging before his readers the views of all the schools of Greek thought in *De Natura Deorum*, and discussing at some length the reasons for believing in the providential effects of divine wisdom and power benevolently wielded. In his *Academics* he considers the case for scepticism. (This treatise provoked Augustine into writing his own *Contra Academicos*.) He also asks what place there can be for philosophical endeavour by later generations when the Greeks have surely said all that is necessary; and tries to divide philosophy in the Platonic way into three areas: the pursuit of truth; the pursuit of of virtue; the study of the natural world and of the mystery of what lies beyond it. Here, too, Augustine was stimulated;[29] he borrows the scheme in the *De Civitate Dei*.

The *Topics*, which was valuable to logicians until the recovery of Aristotle's *Topics*, is also a work of Cicero's maturity. One early work, the *De Inventione*, became by a quirk of its transmission a staple treatise for the early mediaeval study of rhetoric, and in particular for its relevance to the study of argument, and thus of logic.

Macrobius

By reading Cicero the Latin-speaking Christian could thus get a pretty comprehensive picture of at least the outline pattern of ancient Greek thought. Macrobius' *Commentary on the Dream of Scipio* would help further on a number of points. Eriugena seems to have known it. He makes a reference to the question of the location of hell within the circle of the planets and thus 'within the ambit of this world', and comments on the difficulty that the Platonists do not allow for any place outside the cosmos where the soul may experience punishment or enjoy its reward.[30] There is more evidence of the use of Macrobius in the twelfth century. Rupert of Deutz finds it helpful in several places in his *De Trinitate et Operibus Eius*, for example, and it was familiar to many authors who touched on aspects of cosmology.

Macrobius ranges widely in his commentary. He compares Plato and Cicero and considers the claims of a number of other philosophical schools (he was himself opposed to 'the whole faction of the Epicureans'); he discusses the immortality of the soul (I.i.5); he goes into a question always of great mediaeval interest: the use of images and illustrations to convey what is ultimately beyond human grasp, as are the Good, the First Cause, the nature of Ideas; he looks at the idea of boundary in a long discussion of number theory which mediaeval scholars found extremely useful; he explores the way the elements are mixed together to make the world; he discusses the Ciceronian virtues of prudence, temperance, fortitude and justice; he asks whether the soul has a recollection of heaven from the time before its arrival on earth, and what moves the soul (comparing the views of half a dozen ancient philosophers). In all this he takes Cicero much further, and thus provides a substantial reference work on questions of mathematics and natural science as well as upon issues obviously germane to theology.

Boethius

Boethius held a special place as author of both philosophical and Christian writings. For practical purposes his influence must be counted philosophical. The five theological tractates are brief, and had a comparatively brief vogue in the twelfth century, although they were always available to mediaeval scholars. Boethius was mostly read for his logic and for the *Consolation of Philosophy*, and although formidable efforts were made to render the latter Christian, it remained a source of instruction about philosophical ideas above all.

Hermetica

Between the mid-first and late third centuries AD a number of texts ascribed to Hermes Trismegistos came into circulation. They combined elements of Platonic, Neo-Pythagorean and Stoic thought with material drawn from the cults of the East and Near-East,[31] and Gnostic teaching. The end of human life as they saw it was the 'deification' of man, achieved through subjugation of the 'beast' in a man, and cultivation of the spiritual and upwardly aspiring. A taint of magic and astrology hung about these texts as they were drawn on in the Middle Ages. There was also the tell-tale warning sign for orthodox Christians that this was a mystery religion.

Of the hermetic writings the *Asclepius* perhaps occurs most frequently in the Middle Ages. But pseudo-Hermetica were in mediaeval circulation too. The *Secretum Secretorum* was thought to be a work of Aristotle, written for a privileged readership of initiates. Roger Bacon rearranged it, making his own division into books. An unknown Western writer interested in astrology put together a 'hermetic' *Liber Hermetis Mercurii Triplicis de VI Rerum Principiis*, probably in the twelfth century. He drew on current Latin translations of Arabic works on cosmogony and used Adelard of Bath and William of Conches.

The Arabs

We cannot leave the subject of the transmission of classical philosophical texts to the mediaeval West without looking briefly at the work of some of the Arabic philosophers who had commented upon the texts, and whose work sometimes arrived in the West with the translations of the texts themselves from Arabic.

Al-Kindi (d. c.873) knew no Greek, but he used to arrange for others to make translations for him and then improve their Arabic if necessary. He knew Plotinus, but the chief influence upon him was Aristotle. His chief interest as a philosopher was the study of the First Cause, which he thought the proper subject of philosophy at its highest. He had leanings towards natural science too, writing on meteorology, astronomy-and-astrology and music. It is instructive that his list of definitions of philosophy's scope emerges as very close to that of Arnulf Provincialis.[32] His *De Radiis*[33] among other works was, it seems, a strong influence on Roger Bacon, although its teaching was condemned by Giles of Rome in his *Errors of the Philosophers* about 1270, and the general condemnation of 1277 includes at least one of Al-Kindi's doctrines.

Al-Farabi (?879–?950) contributed material on the proof of the existence of the First Principle of all things, and on the theory of emanation, and in the area of the theory of knowledge, as well as commentaries on Aristotle which were used in the West from the late twelfth century. Avicenna (980–1037) wrote on the soul, and on the metaphysics of Aristotle. He dealt with the problem of universals, with proofs of the existence of God, the theory of emanation, the hierarchy of being, providence, and the problem of evil, topics especially relevant to the Platonic heritage, but discussed with a strongly Aristotelian bias by him. His work was known in the West by the beginning of the thirteenth century.

Averroes (1126–98) was especially influential because controversial. He, like Avicenna, wrote on proofs of the existence of God, on God's knowledge and problems of epistemology, on the theory of emanation, and on the intellect. Like that of Avicenna, his Aristotelianism was deeply dyed with Platonism, because parts of Plotinus' *Enneads* were known to him under the title of *The Theology of Aristotle* and he believed the paraphrase of Proclus known as the *Liber de Causis* to be a work of Aristotle, too. A row was generated in the thirteenth century over the interpretation placed by Siger of Brabant upon Averroes' teaching about the intellect. Averroes seemed to him to be saying in his commentary on Aristotle's *De Anima* that the potential intellect is one and the same in all rational beings. That would have implications for the relationship of human mind to the mind of God which were unacceptable to the defenders of orthodoxy, and indeed the Averroist position was condemned in 1270 by the Bishop of Paris, prompted a vigorous exchange of treatises between Aquinas and the 'Averroists'.

3

KNOWING AND LANGUAGE

THEOLOGY AND PHILOSOPHICAL METHOD

We have touched already on the question of the use theologians felt it proper to make of the methods developed by classical philosophers. There were fundamental problems here to do with the ways in which human understanding comes by what it knows, and conveys it to others. Christians recognised two gifts which did not come into the philosophers' reckoning: revelation in Holy Scripture; and the gift of faith which is inseparable from trust on the part of the believer. 'I believe' is not identical with 'I know.' But there was also a substantial common heritage of epistemology and methodology, with which both philosophy and theology had to deal.

A doctrine of divine illumination was acceptable to both philosophers and Christians in the first Christian centuries. Thought was regarded by Plato as a kind of 'seeing' in the light thrown from above upon the mind. Gregory the Great was fond of speaking of 'the mind's eye' (*oculus mentis*), and the expression passed into common Western usage. This illumination was understood in several ways in mediaeval Western Christian thought.[1] First and foremost, it was the light of faith, shed on men and women so that they might believe. Sometimes (Anselm, *Proslogion*, 1) it was a blinding light, into which one must go in trust and trembling. But it showed where to look, and it was the means by which God's people were to know him. Secondly, it was the insight by which truth is recognised, and which we make use of when we say that something is 'self-evident'.[2] William of Auxerre (d. 1231) thought illumination was needed before it was possible to 'see' first principles in this way.[3] Thirdly, it provided a means of assessing and identifying the evidence brought into the mind through the senses. This was an area explored by Augustine at the end of his *Confessions*, and we find the theme recurring throughout the Middle Ages as scholars debated the problem of universals.

This third area in which divine illumination might be deemed to play a part was not characteristically discussed in the Middle Ages in connection with a theory of language and signs which Augustine set out in the *De Doctrina Christiana* and which it was necessary to harmonise with the accounts given by Aristotle in the *De Interpretatione* and by the Roman grammarians. Augustine begins from the natural signs which are to be found in the world (smoke which tells us that there is a fire), and signs which are accepted by convention, such as gestures which convey an attitude or a response. Words are conventional signs too, which are necessary like gestures because as sinful beings we cannot see clearly into one another's minds. Augustine argues in the *De Magistro* (VIII.21) that this system of signs depends on God's gift of the ideas to which they refer; God puts the ideas into our heads and illuminates them for us so that we can see them; we learn to associate with them certain signs, so that when the sign is perceived the idea is brought to mind. Thus we do not learn from signs, not even from words. We can only convey and receive by signs what we already 'know', in the sense that when presented with it we are able to recognise it. Inner knowledge is all-important, God's help indispensable and signs, linguistic or otherwise, mere servants.

They serve by signifying. It was the signifying function of words in particular which preoccupied mediaeval scholarship more consistently than perhaps any other topic in the study of the *artes* of grammar, logic and rhetoric. Augustine looked into the matter briefly in his *De Magistro*. There, in a dialogue, he and his son Adeodatus discuss a line of the *Aeneid* (II.659) word by word, asking what each word signifies. Their purpose is to discover whether it is true that every word must signify in order to be a word at all, as was Aristotle's view. In the *De Interpretatione* he distinguishes words from mere sounds by their power of signifying. A true word is a *vox significativa*. Augustine and his son proceed comfortably enough until they come to the word *nihil*. How can *nihil* signify something if what it signifies is 'nothing'? (This nice little puzzle was taken up again by the Carolingian scholar Fredegisus.)[4] The Roman grammarians also held that it is the function of words to signify. There was an important disagreement between Priscian, who thought nouns signify both substance and quality (K II.55.6) and Aristotle–Boethius, for whom paronyms such as *albus*, 'white', signify only quality (*PL* 64.194). Both the problem about the signification of *nihil* and the discrepancy between Priscian and Aristotle–Boethius over denominatives interested Anselm, who touched on the first in his *De Casu Diaboli* (S 1.249) and wrote a treatise on the second (the *De Grammatico*). It was at this level of small misfits in the piecing together of the Augustinian, grammarian and Aristotle–Boethian traditions that discussion about signification was generated up to the twelfth century. Then, with the greater availability of the textbooks and the heightening of interest in the study of the *artes* in the burgeoning schools, there were significant developments in both epistemology in general and signification theory in particular.

Thinking about things

How do the objects of thought enter the mind? In Book X of *The Confessions* Augustine gives a detailed account of his own experience and tries to explain it. He begins from the senses. The soul perceives by means of the senses those things which it is the special province of each sense to feel. It admits through many separate 'entrances' memories of what is perceived, so that everything is classified as it enters the memory. He notes it as important that the things themselves do not enter the memory by this process; it is rather that images of them are formed. Once something has been perceived and stored it becomes possible to recall its image to mind at will and to reflect upon it in an orderly way, without its becoming confused with other images. But images can be combined again, at will, so that one may reconstruct complex past events or project future ones as though they were present (*Confessions* X.7–10).

The memory does not hold only what has been introduced into it through sense-perception. Augustine can remember much (if not all) of facts which he has learned through being told them in words. These he believed not because he had direct evidence of them (that is, the prompting of sense), but because something in his own mind recognised them to be true. He infers from this that they were in some way already stored in the recesses of his memory, but so deep down that had no one awakened them for him, he might never have known that they were there (*Confessions* X.12). He realises that his mind can handle all this on more than one level. He can recall arguments for and against certain opinions and know that he knows what he knows, which shows that there is a yet higher faculty in his soul which watches his thought-processes at work; it also allows him to distance himself from recollected sensation to the point where he can, for example, speak of physical pain without actually experiencing the pain again, and yet understand what he speaks of (*Confessions* X.14–15).

The Platonism in which Augustine was steeped, and which he continued to respect as a Christian, consistently saw the body as an obstacle to the soul in its striving to perceive directly those things beyond sense in which reality supremely consists. Augustine, however, argues that the perceptions of the senses, though bodily, are a God-given aid to the soul's understanding, and a means by which it may ascend towards the knowledge of God himself. There was some Platonic support for this interpretation in Plato's later works, and in the teaching of some later Platonists we find the notion that since the world the senses perceive is itself in some way a likeness of the higher reality, it can be used as a pointer to it. A hierarchy of images is envisaged contemporaneously with, or a little after, Augustine by Proclus and Ps.-Dionysius, but it is already to be found in Philo. Philo teaches that the sensible world is the image of the Logos, and the Logos himself the image of the Father.

Mediaeval versions of Augustine's account of a progression from sense-perception by way of image-making and abstraction to a truly spiritual and rational encounter with the mind of God are to be found in, for instance, Anselm's *Monologion* and Bonaventure's *Itinerarium Mentis ad Deum*; but the notion is widely diffused in many authors.

Talking about things

The first difficulty concerns the relationship between the metaphysical structure of reality and the structure of reality as language seemingly supposes it to be. The assumption on which Augustine and the Platonists proceeded was that particular objects perceptible to the senses which can conveniently be labelled with words are substances secondary to forms, ideas and universals, which are themselves dependent upon a divine reality. This metaphysics is reversed by the practice of grammarians and logicians, for whom the naming of particulars naturally comes first.[5] It is not even necessary for grammarians and logicians to postulate the actual existence of any generality or universal to make language work. William of Conches, writing as a twelfth-century grammarian, says in his commentary on Priscian that proper names signify particular substances with their individual qualities. If we want to use a name to signify a universal substance we simply understand it to signify a common quality, so that such a term will do for any individual of that sort. William believes that it is not necessary for any such general thing to exist for it to be possible to use words intelligibly in this way. For the logicians, Boethius had said in writing on the *Isagoge* of Porphyry (and indebted to Alexander of Aphrodisias) that universals are thoughts which have a derivation from the nature of things which can be perceived by the senses.

It is an irony that although Boethius thought it did not matter for practical purposes whether or not 'things-in-general' actually exist, he set in train centuries of mediaeval endeavour to settle the point. For mediaeval grammarians and logicians the problem which it was a practical necessity to solve was the complex one of the significative behaviour of words. A word must have an *impositio*, a primary signification, or it cannot be a word at all, for words are distinguished from mere sounds by being significant. It may have several such impositions, and then it will be equivocal. Porphyry agrees with Scripture in describing a particular occasion when all names of first imposition were given to things, as Adam named the animals. But the same word-form may have more than one signification in a different way, where one signification is on a different level from another. If I say 'Peter is a man', I am using 'man' to refer to the species, not to the individual. Or I may use 'man' differently again when I say that '"man" is a noun', or differently again in saying '"man" is a word of one syllable'. It is a relatively straightforward matter to indicate what is happening in modern typography by using inverted commas. But the Stoics struggled to identify these differences without such aids, and in the mediaeval Latin West it was necessary to resort to devices involving a special technical vocabulary, in which higher-order significations are called *nominationes* or *appellationes*. It became important to determine the 'supposition', that is, the particular way in which a word was being used in a given context, so that first impositions should not be confused with other impositions.

The recognition that the context in which a word is used makes a difference to its signification proved to be of supreme importance in the development of 'terminist' logic from the end of the twelfth century.[6] The first step was to reconcile Aristotle's rule that there is no need to look beyond nouns and verbs in classifying parts of speech with the eight parts of speech identified by the Roman grammarians. This was done by distinguishing 'categorematic' words, that is, words which signify in their own right (nouns and verbs, which signify substances), from words which signify only in conjunction with categorematic terms. These *syncategoremata* are prepositions, conjunctions, adverbs, and so on.[7]

When syncategorematic words are brought into play it becomes natural to take the *propositio* rather than the component words as the basic unit of meaning. The problem which now becomes interesting is that of the relationship between the meaning which is the word's *essentia* or *forma* (which must always lie behind the signification it carries in a particular context because it is its natural property); and the notion that it is the whole proposition together which signifies. To this was added the question we have already met, whether what is signified must be true or really exist in order to be signified at all. A favourite schoolroom example here was the use of the word *chimaera* to signify an animal agreed to be mythical. At a deeper level the issue includes the case of universals and the question whether we could speak of them at all if they did not exist.

By the second half of the thirteenth century the terminists who had pioneered work in these areas were beginning to give way to 'modists'. Modist logicians explored not only 'modes of signifying' (*modi significandi*), but also 'modes of understanding' (*modi intelligendi*) and 'modes of being' (*modi essendi*) (all of this being envisaged as in line with the three operations of the soul described by Aristotle in the *De Anima*). They asked whether words could lose their signification and whether there can exist classes with no members, and other questions designed to challenge existing explanations.

What are things-in-general?

The problem of universals, then, was for practical purposes inseparable in the twelfth century from the technical work on the operation of logic and language which was taking Aristotle's logic much further, and which created a speculative grammar over and above the groundwork laid by Priscian and Donatus. The *logica moderna* constituted a substantial advance in the field, to a degree not matched perhaps by any other branch of mediaeval philosophy. It produced a body of textbooks (the *Logica Moderna*) which were not mere commentary on Aristotle but which broke new ground.

The problem of universals itself arose in part for mediaeval students of the *artes* from Boethius' comments on *De Interpretatione* 3.16[b]19.[8] When it signifies, a word makes someone think of something. It can thus be said to cause something to be thought of, to have an effect upon the mind. A similar chain of causation can be traced in the way a written word evokes a spoken word and the spoken word a word in the mind (Boethius, on *De Int.* I.16[a]13[8] and Augustine, *De Trinitate* XV.10). It was difficult not to read into this 'causation' view of signification the assumption that the effects caused must have some real existence. Most twelfth-century thinkers were in some sense 'realists' about the existence of mental words (the notorious late eleventh-century and early twelfth-century Roscelin of Compiègne, and perhaps Abelard, being exceptions). Most would also (paradoxically) take the view that mental words are of a higher order of reality than spoken or written words, and that, *a fortiori*, those mental words we call universals or species are of a higher order of reality than words for particular things and the particular things to which they refer. At one extreme it was held that universals are distinct things in their own right; more moderate scholars would say that a universal exists at least as a substance which can be found in the essence of all particular things of its kind. At the least it could be held that, say, two men or two horses have a like 'humanity' or 'horseness'. Then a universal or species might be regarded as a collective thing, made up of all its particulars. Or one might describe genera and species as 'sorts of things' (for which the technical term was *maneries*). The 'causative' notion is detectable once more in Gilbert of Poitiers' again controversial twelfth-century attempt to distinguish between that which a particular thing is and that 'by which' it is (in the case of a particular man, his humanity). He tried to resolve the question of the real existence of the *quo est* by arguing that no *quo est* can exist except through a *quod est*, that is, through the particular thing; while the *quod est* cannot itself exist except by that (universal or species) by which it exists (*quo est*). This became controversial when Gilbert tried to apply it to the case of God. If we say that *Deus* exists *divinitate*, 'by divinity', it seems possible that we are saying that something called 'divinity' is being postulated as the cause of God himself.

Peter Abelard drew on both Augustine and Aristotle–Boethius in his own account of these issues. He describes how the senses respond to what they perceive; the imagination can recall in the form of pictures in the mind things once perceived by the senses even if they are not present; the intellect classifies into genera and species. Thus he modifies Augustine's notion that the very portals through which sense-impressions enter the memory are classificatory pigeon-holes. Using Boethius on the *De Interpretatione*, Abelard goes on to suggest that the intellect produces thoughts which it derives from images. It seems important to him here that there can be images of things which do not exist, mere fictions, and he is willing to infer from this that there is no need to postulate real existence for universals either. For Abelard images are nothings, with neither form nor substance. Words are related to ideas by producing them in the minds of hearers (as Boethius says). Words are related to things by signifying them, but they do no more when they signify than provide a means of talking about things. Statements or propositions merely designate the way in which the things signified by the categorematic terms are related to one another. When a term such as 'man' is used with universal reference, it merely tells us what men have in common.

The debate on universals reopened in earnest in the thirteenth century, when the study of Aristotle's book *On the Soul* made it fashionable to look towards the forms of things in the world external to the mind as the source of thoughts in the mind. Aristotle suggests that the mind is informed with the thought in a way analogous with the manner in which the senses are themselves affected when they feel. The emphasis shifted in part away from the twelfth-century preoccupation with universals in connection with the theory of language, and towards a wider treatment, in which the behaviour of language has to be accounted for alongside the physics and metaphysics of the matter. Aquinas, for example, looked at the way in which quantities, because they are finite, introduce some sort of individuality into universal matter. Duns Scotus would answer that there must be something which causes general natures somehow to 'contract' into particulars.

The comparatively straightforward 'realism' of the twelfth century was thus subtly modified in the thirteenth and fourteenth centuries. Duns Scotus, for example, suggested that each thing may be regarded as having a 'nature', which can be defined as 'the sort of thing it is'. This nature is not either singular or universal in itself. But it has a universal character in the mind, when the intellect holds it as a concept. William of Ockham disliked this solution because it seemed to him to imply that universals are based on something which really exists, outside the intellect. An alternative 'realist' hypothesis, also disliked by Ockham, was that a universal is a formal distinction, which pretends, for purposes of thinking about them, that things which are really one thing are more than one thing. For example, one might think of a white house that it is white, and that it is a house. The universals 'whiteness' and 'houseness' have to be distinguished if we are to think clearly. But we understand that there are not two things, a white and a house, but one. Even the acceptance of a formal existence for universals was too much for Ockham. He held that everything which really exists in particular, and only words or mental concepts can be universal. For the older, Aristotle-derived, view that things which really exist cause thoughts in the mind (from which it is to be inferred that thoughts are of real things), he substituted the idea that a thought in the mind (*ficta*) 'stands for' (*supposit*) a thing in the world. From this he infers the notion that thoughts are merely acts of supposition, and when such an act takes place, all that happens is that the thought informs the mind, rather as whiteness informs a white thing. We use words to stand for single individuals or for classes. We can do the same in thought. There is no need, says Ockham, to regard the classes as having any independent or 'real' existence.

ARRIVING AT THE TRUTH

The theologian must be able, like the student of any other discipline, to distinguish truth from falsehood and to prove a disputed point. It was a commonplace of the encyclopaedists that it was supremely the province of logic to distinguish truth from falsehood, although it might be more accurate to say that logic deals in validity of inference. Mediaeval scholars made use of the instruments of formal reasoning to establish conclusions in every discipline. Yet reasoning must have matter to work on. The propositions from which syllogisms are constructed can be seen to lead to true conclusions only if they themselves are shown to be true.

There were broadly two ways in which a proposition could be tested. The first depended on its being self-evidently true, or capable of demonstration from a self-evident truth. That brings us into the immensely complex area of the mediaeval theory of topics.

In his *Posterior Analytics* Aristotle speaks of the first principles on which all sciences must rest and discusses whether each sphere of knowledge must have first principles peculiar to itself, which define it as a science. Euclid, in his *Elements of Geometry*, makes use of axioms as the starting-points for demonstration. These are, by definition, themselves indemonstrable. They rest upon their self-evident truth. Geometry is unique among the sciences, as Plato perhaps recognised, in its capacity for demonstration from first principles in this way, but the elegance and cogency of the demonstrative method gave it strong appeal to mediaeval scholars who wanted to provide the strongest possible proof, especially in matters of theology.

Before demonstration can proceed it is necessary to be sure of the first principles on which it is to be built. Here the mediaeval heritage was complex and to some degree confusing. Aristotle's *Posterior Analytics* was not in use until the late twelfth century. Before its arrival, discussion turned on Cicero and Boethius, with, from the mid-twelfth century, some notion of Euclid's contribution.[9] Cicero writes as a rhetorician familiar with both logicians' and rhetoricians' use of 'topics' (*loci*) in the Roman world. For the orator a 'topic' may be no more than an illustrative story, an anecdote, an *exemplum*, brought in to support a contention. For the logician it is a maxim or axiom of some sort.[10] Boethius commented on Cicero's *Topics*, and wrote a monograph on the difference between dialectical and rhetorical use of *topoi*, but he did not transmit to the early Middle Ages any direct knowledge of Aristotle's *Topics*. Boethius realised that Cicero's *loci* are not strictly axioms or individual first principles, but rather classes of axioms. He also noted a difference which was to be the first importance to mediaeval theory, between 'dialectical' arguments, in which the axioms that form the premisses or propositions of a syllogism do not have to the self-evidently true but only inherently probable; and 'demonstrative' arguments, in which they must be self-evidently true.

Boethius made a further significant contribution to this discussion, in a work which falls outside his group of logical textbooks. In the *De Hebdomadibus* he discusses the notion of beginning from self-evidence truths (*communis animi conceptiones*) and proceeding to build up on them other truths which will be accepted by everyone as soon as it is shown how they depend on first principles. It is noteworthy that the phrase *communis animi conceptio* was used by the twelfth-century translators of Euclid to render his 'axiom'. Boethius does not in fact continue in a Euclidean way in the *De Hebdomadibus*. Instead, he tantalises the reader by leaving it to him to work out which of the listed axioms supports the argument at each point, and the twelfth-century commentators on the *De Hebdomadibus* spent a good deal of effort in trying to agree on the solution to the puzzle.

What, then, is the status of the axioms of theology which we call 'articles of faith'? Alan of Lille discussed various contemporary viewpoints. Some say that faith is a general perception of invisible things which pertain to the Christian religion (*ad Christianam religionem pertinentium*). An article of faith is a particular perception of a specific thing, for example, of the Nativity of Christ or his Passion. Some say that the Nativity, Passion, and so on are themselves the articles of faith, not faith's perception of them. Others, Alan among them, think that 'invisible' means 'intelligible'. That is to say, the events themselves were visible when they occurred, but there was in the Nativity and the Passion and the other *eventus* on which faith rests some invisible truth beyond ordinary human perception. An example is the union of divine and human nature in Christ.[11] This notion of the presence of an element of mystery, a profound truth too deep to be immediately self-evident to human reason,[12] is important in connection with the special problems posed by the articles of faith.

Alan of Lille and his younger contemporary Nicholas of Amiens made ambitious attempts to work out a whole system of Christian theology from a set of axioms, Alan in his *Regulae Theologicae* and Nicholas in a *De Fide Catholica*. Alan kept to what may be called a 'Boethian' pattern. He took a first axiom and tried to draw others out of it in a stream, introducing new principles as he needed them. Nicholas proceeded in a Euclidean way, beginning with axioms, postulates and definitions, constructing theorems, and using theorems already demonstrated as the first principles of later demonstrations.[13] Both found that things went relatively smoothly while they were dealing with the topics of the Boethian *theologia*, but that topics like redemption, Church and sacraments presented difficulties of another order.

Alan of Lille died in 1202. He was thus one of the last major scholars of the period before Aristotle's *Libri naturales* became generally available in the West, and his set of theological axioms therefore have some importance as evidence of what could be done with philosophy in theology's service before Aristotle's controversial assistance was brought more fully into play in Paris and elsewhere.

In his Prologue Alan explains what he understands by a *regula*. Every science rests on its rules as on foundations. The 'maxims' of dialectic, the 'commonplaces' of rhetoric, the 'general opinions' of ethics, and so on are all peculiar to their proper disciplines. Alan does not base this doctrine on Aristotle's *Posterior Analytics* but on the authority of Boethius' *De Hebdomadibus*, which had been comprehensively commented on in the schools of northern France in his youth. He is attracted to Boethius by his acknowledgement that the [h]ebdomades are profoundly mysterious, of a depth and majesty which means that they are not for beginners. Boethius' *communis animi conceptiones* are self-evident truths, and therefore indemonstrable. Some of them are grasped by everyone. Others are intelligible only to those few who are able to understand deeper truths. Theological *regulae* seem to Alan to be of the latter kind, and he proposes to deal with 'these which scarcely anyone knows'. There is, then, an element of mystery necessary to Alan's scheme which Aristotle could not provide for, although the *Posterior Analytics* had been available for several generations when Alan wrote.

During the early thirteenth-century crisis over the introduction of the new Aristotle at Paris, William of Auxerre dismissed the idea that he might 'use the words of Aristotle as giving authentic proof' (*'tamquam authenticis ad probationem*'). That is no more than employing a dialectical topic. It can furnish only probable proof, and one can base no more than opinion on it. His plan is to arrive at demonstrative certainty wherever he can. But in practice, systematic attempts at proof by demonstration alone were rare. They were too difficult. Theology did not lend itself to the method (any more than politics proved to do, when Dante attempted it in his *De Monarchia*). In practice, theologians proceeded by making a mixture of propositions which could be claimed to rest on their pure reasonableness and propositions which depended on authorities for their acceptability. A glance at Aquinas' *Summae* will make the point. Most often authorities are Scriptural (and thus carry direct divine warrant), or patristic (and thus carry very considerable weight as the words of Fathers of the Church).

In practice classical philosophical texts are also used throughout our period as sources which can be quoted in support of an argument. Often reservations are expressed, and it is always understood that a philosopher will never outweigh Scripture (even where his standing is high in general), if at some point he contradicts that explicit teaching of the Bible. Roger Bacon sees a need to explain that it is necessary for practical reasons for Christian theologians to cite philosophical authorities in his own day. 'The principal occupation of theologians today is to treat questions; and the greater part of all questions has to do with the terms used by philosophy . . . the remainder, which is concerned with the terms theology employs, is itself discussed by means of the authorities and arguments and solutions of philosophy, as all educated people know.'[14] He himself was always willing to 'bring in the testimonies of the philosophers' *in theologicis*, but he finds it politic to insist that the ones he uses are worthy examples, *autentica*.

Bacon's insistence on this point reflects much contemporary anxiety. He tries in his *Opus Maius* to give a systematic account of the issues. One may say of a philosopher as one may not of a Biblical author that he is a fallible and imperfect authority. Even Aristotle, who was, says Bacon, the wisest of the philosophers, was sometimes in error (I.iii). We should respect the achievement of those who pursued truth by the light of human understanding in the earliest ages, even if we can see that they have not been wholly successful (I.v). Here Bacon is apparently trying to strike a balance between that over-enthusiastic citation of philosophical authorities which was bringing some of his contemporaries into conflict with theologians; and the alternative of rejecting all philosophers out of hand as unworthy or mistaken.

He argued more than once that later generations are in a better position than earlier ones to see where the truth lies and to judge where their predecessors went wrong. The first seekers after truth had no help. Those who come after them had only their aid. But *semper crevit sapientia* (wisdom has grown), and bit by bit knowledge has been added to. We inherit the results of the labours of all who went before us (Bacon, *Metaphysica*, p. 5; see also *Opus Maius* I.vi). In the twelfth century a similar view had been put more modestly by Bernard of Chartres, who is reported (by John of Salisbury, a former pupil) to have said that the modern scholar is like a dwarf sitting on the shoulders of the giants of old. He can see further than they could, but not because he is greater than they; quite the contrary. This gives us a double standard for the rating of the authority of secular authors and in particular for that of philosophers. On the one hand, they can be seen as persons of limited attainments, so that we now know better than they; on the other, they can be regarded as figures of great dignity, giants whose like no longer strides the land, and thus as authoritative for the purposes of quotation in support of an argument.

Aquinas asks whether a master who is deciding theological questions ought to use reasoning or authorities more. It is argued that in every science questions are best decided by the first principles of that science. But the first principles of the science of theology are articles of faith, which are made known to us by authorities. So it would seem that theological questions ought chiefly to be decided by authorities. On the other hand, Titus 1.9 can be read as an endorsement of the use of reasoning to clear up contradictions. Aquinas' own opinion is that one should decide the matter by keeping the end in view. To remove doubts, authorities are best, and they should be chosen so as to convince the individuals concerned. For example, Jews will be convinced best by Old Testament texts. When the task in hand is one of teaching, as is the case in the schools, reasoning is best. If the Master uses nothing but 'bare authorities' he will certainly show the listener the truth, but the listener will not grow in understanding and so he will learn nothing (*Quodlibet* IV.q.ix.a.3).

Part II

4

GOD

PROVING THE EXISTENCE OF GOD

Augustine had demonstrated from the ascending order of excellence in the universe that there must be a God.[1] That was an exercise with a character and purpose closely in tune with that of Anselm in the *Monologion*, which he called a 'meditation on the Divine Being' (*essentia*) (Preface). It may be, he begins, that there is someone who does not know of the one Nature (*natura*), the Highest of all things which have being (*summa omnium quae sunt*), alone sufficient to itself in its eternal beatitude (*beatitudo*), giving and causing, through its own omnipotent goodness (Chapter 1). Anselm hazards the possibility that there is not only someone who does not know but even someone who does not believe that this is so. He promises that even the unbeliever can be won round by reasoning. But the tone of the promise is that of a master among friends and pupils, a monastic superior among his monks, engaged in a philosophical meditation together in a context of faith and prayer. The purpose is to heighten faith, and ground it in intellectual apprehension, not to win to faith recalcitrant or slow minds. It is of the first importance here that Anselm's Highest is described in one breath as not only existing but omnipotent, good, sufficient to itself and the source of the being of all creatures. There is, as it were, a package, Neoplatonically made up, in which the existence of God comes with certain inseparable attributes. It is important in reading Anselm's ontological argument to recognise that the same is true of the *Proslogion* proof. In the Preface to the *Proslogion*, Anselm explains that he had become dissatisfied with the arguments of the *Monologion*, not because he now thought them unsound, but because they were inelegantly strung together as if in a chain. He had since been looking for a single argument which would prove not only that God truly exists (*quia uia Deus vere est*), but also all the other concomitant truths in the 'package', that he is the Highest Good, needs no other, and is the source of the being and well-being of all creatures, and whatever else we believe about the divine Being (*substantia*). The *vere* is perhaps important. It implies, as had the hypothetical character of the person in the *Monologion* requiring a rational demonstration, that we are dealing here with the meditations of the faithful rather than with the convincing of unbelievers. Everything about the *Proslogion*'s construction suggests as much, its opening chapter of prayer and the interludes throughout in which, like Augustine in the *Confessions*, Anselm addresses God directly in gratitude or supplication.

It is for this reason that we must say that, in a sense, Anselm only 'appears' to be seeking to prove the existence of God. We have not yet arrived at a situation comparable with that which confronted eighteenth-century apologists, for whom the individual who denies that there is a God is not a literary fiction, the 'Fool' of the Psalms, but a person who really needs to be convinced.

Anselm's originality lies in the structure of the *Proslogion* argument itself. In the *Monologion* he had proceeded in roughly Augustine's way, to lead the reader from his own direct knowledge of good things in the world to infer the existence of a common and higher Good from which they all derived, and from which they draw that which is good in themselves. The hierarchy of excellence and the notion that some one thing must stand at the top of it are indispensable to this argument. It enables Anselm to show that the supreme Nature exists through itself and has no prior cause (*Monologion*, 1–6). He is able to go on from there and demonstrate both the basic Christian principles of creation: that God made all things from nothing, although he had had the ideas which give them their form in his mind from all eternity; and that he sustains his creation in being (Chapters 7–14). He is also able to show that God is supreme Justice, without beginning and end, immutable, omnipresent and yet in no place or time (Chapters 16–25).

In the *Proslogion* he makes an entirely fresh use of the hierarchy of excellence. God may be described as 'that than which nothing greater can be thought'. We begin at the top of the ladder of understanding up which Anselm invited us to climb in the *Monologion*. He forces us to confront the question whether what we think of as God must, because it thus lies at the ultimate limit of an understanding which is itself attainable only when thought aspires to the highest, be more than a thought. It is self-evidently true that if 'that than which nothing greater can be thought' exists in reality as well as in the mind, it is in fact greater than a 'that than which nothing greater can be thought' which is only in the mind. If there is not only a possibility we can think of, but also a self-evident truth about that possibility, Anselm would argue that to say that God exists only in thought must involve a contradiction. 'That than which a greater cannot be thought' would not be 'that than which a greater cannot be thought', for we have thought of a greater. Since that is manifestly impossible, Anselm says that there can be no doubt that 'that than which a greater cannot be thought' exists both in the understanding and in reality (*et in intellectu et in re*) (*Proslogion*, 2). He develops the principle in his next chapter. If it were possible to think that this 'that than which a greater cannot be thought' did not exist, then it would manifestly not be 'that than which a greater cannot be thought', for it would not be being thought at all. There remains the Fool, who appears to be doing the impossible, when he says in his heart that there is no God (Psalms 13.1, 52.1). We must distinguish, says Anselm, between thinking mere words and thinking the thing which the words signify. The Fool might think the words, but he could not think the thing (Chapter 4). Anselm can now apply his reasoning to all the other things we believe about God, as he promised (*Proemium*). God is whatever it is than not to be, just, truthful, happy, and so on, as can be proved in the same way as his very existence (Chapters 5ff.).

It is important that God's existence is never fully separated in Anselm's mind, or in Anselm's system, from the complement of ultimately Platonic assumptions about the divine nature with which it is accompanied in Augustine and in Anselm's own earlier *Monologion*. We are dealing with a Being which has of its substance a number of attributes. It was Gaunilo, monk of Marmoutiers, who insisted that the nub of the matter was the argument for God's actual existence. He wrote a reply to Anselm in the person of the Fool, contending that he for one could think that which Anselm said it was impossible to think. He suggested that if Anselm's argument were sound, it would also be true that the most beautiful island one could think of would necessarily exist in reality as well as in imagination, and so on for the best of everything. Anselm was pleased with this subtle response, and thought the point worth answering. He instructed that Gaunilo's reply and his own rejoinder to it should be inserted at the end of the copies of the *Proslogion* thereafter. His answer was that God must be unique in being of such a kind that his existence can be proved by Anselm's argument.

Gilbert Crispin, one of Anselm's monks at Bec and later abbot of Westminster, made some use of Anselm's formula, but with the difference that he preferred to describe God as 'that than which a *better* cannot be thought'. But we have to wait for Aquinas to take up Anselm's argument again and criticise it fully. He saw that the *Proslogion* argument falls into a class by itself. He considers it apart from other arguments, under the question whether the existence of God is self-evident (*ST* I.q.2.a.1). In Objection 1 he summarises Anselm's argument in Chapter 2 of the *Proslogion* and replies to it by saying that Anselm makes an unjustified leap from thought to reality. It must also be conceded, Aquinas argues, that those who deny that God exists demonstrate by their position that the existence of God is not self-evident. Whether or not Aquinas put his finger on a real weakness, it is certainly the case that Anselm did not succeed in settling the matter of God's existence once and for all. But on the other hand, his argument has never been decisively refuted, because it has proved impossible to determine on exactly what it turns. It is of some importance here that it hangs upon precisely the question of that intersection between thought and reality which was central to mediaeval work on epistemology and language.

William of Conches made an early attempt at a type of proof of the existence of God which Aquinas was to exploit more fully in the *Summa Theologiae*, and which has respectable philosophical ancestry. William argues that to move at all, bodies must be animated by spirits. Spirit would not join itself to body unless some powerful agent caused it to do so, and held it in its relationship to body. No creature could have the necessary wisdom to do that. So we must postulate the existence of a Creator. Aquinas constructs five proofs which depend in various ways upon reasoning back from an observable effect in the created world to a Creator. Some things are visibly in motion. Whatever is moved must be moved by a mover. But there cannot be an infinite regression of movers, for then there would be no movement at all, because no initial impetus. Therefore there must be a First Mover, and that is God. In a similar way, Aquinas argues from effects to causes, to a chain of causes, and thence to the necessity for a First Cause. Thirdly, he suggests, we may take the fact that in the created world, where there is generation and corruption, it is always possible for things not to be. If there were nothing whose being was necessary, a situation might arise when all possible existences at once were not, and so there would be nothing in existence at all. If that happened it would not have been possible for anything to come into existence, because nothing could have brought anything into existence. He completes the third proof by explaining that if we postulate not only one but a chain of such necessary existences, one dependent upon the next, we must, as in the case of the Prime Mover and the First Cause, come ultimately to a Necessary Being which has its being of no other, and which is God. The fourth proof is of the 'hierarchy of excellence' kind. Aquinas argues that to say that something is more or less good, true, and so on is to say that it resembles to a particular degree something which is the best and greatest. He cites (as Augustine and Anselm were not in a position to do in their versions of this argument) Aristotle's *Metaphysics* (II.i, 993ᵇ30): what is greatest in truth is also greatest in being. In any class of things there must be something, he says, which is the cause of everything in that class. Aristotle says a little earlier in the *Metaphysics*, for example, that fire, which is the maximum of all heat, is the cause of all hot things (II.i, 993ᵇ25). Aquinas reasons that there must be something which is the cause of being, goodness and every other perfection in all things, and this is God. A fifth proof can be drawn from the governance of all things. Natural bodies act as if for a purpose, and yet where there is no sentience, there can be no self-determination. There is clearly an intelligence in charge, an archer directing the arrow, and this is God (*ST* I.q.2.a.3).

The mediaeval essays in proving the existence of God need to be set in the context of a question which was of much more frequent interest to the classical philosophers: what is to be said of his 'being'.

TALKING ABOUT DIVINE BEING

It was of concern to generations of Platonists that nothing should be predicated of the supremely divine which might in any way imply diminishment or limit, or be construed as so doing. For some, that meant placing God even beyond being, or at least declaring that to say that he *is*, is not to say of him anything which tells us *what he is*.[2] Alternatively, some thought it allowable to speak of God's being, if his Being was clearly distinguished from the sort of being possible to things in the world of sense, or even the intelligible world.[3] This kind of refinement was possible in Greek thought in part because the Greek language allowed it to be expressed. Latin's comparative *inopia verborum*, at least until the later mediaeval centuries, made anxiety less acute on this point for Latin-speakers. For Anselm of Canterbury it was enough to seek to prove 'that God truly is' ('*quia deus vere est*');[4] he had no anxiety that to do so would be to predicate of God something unworthy of him. The terms *ens, essentia, existentia, subsistentia* had not yet acquired their later mediaeval technical loading. He is able to say that *ens* is equivalent to *existens* or *subsistens*, and that *essentia* bears the same relationship to *esse* and *ens* as *lux* does to *lucere* and *lucens* (*Monologion*, 5, S.1.20.15–16). He predicates all three of the Godhead, with clear Trinitarian connotations. Even for Aquinas the burning questions are not to do with whether we may speak of God's being at all, but whether God's existence is self-evident and whether it can be demonstrated (*ST* I.q.2.aa.1,2).

Underlying what were for Christians theological questions about the use of particular terms for, or concepts of, being in relation to God were the primarily philosophical matters dealt with by Aristotle in the *Metaphysics*. Aristotle suggests that there is a science which studies being as being. From the late twelfth century Avicenna's *Metaphysics* was available in Latin, and Averroes' commentary on Aristotle's *Metaphysics* could be read in Latin from the early thirteenth century. Avicenna argues that metaphysics cannot prove that God exists, because that would make it a self-referent science, attempting the impossible, that is, to prove the existence of what it is about. Averroes thought the task of proving the existence of God belonged to physics, not metaphysics, because physics can prove that there must be a Prime Mover.

A lengthy debate took place in the thirteenth-century schools about this problem and the related one of whether essence, being and existence are the same thing, and if not, how they are connected. Here God presents the central problem, for it seems that if he exists, essence and existence must be one in him. But a tempting array of subsidiary problems arose, about essence and existence in created things. Henri de Gand[5] was drawn to the Averroist account and he tried to explore the connection between being, on the one hand, and goodness, truth, unity, on the other, as essential properties of things and therefore not in any sense 'added' to them. He argues that if being were some sort of superadded *esse*, it is hard to see what it would be (Substance? Matter? Form? Accident?). Giles of Rome took up the questions which arise here about 'substance', 'matter', 'bodies' and 'quantities'.

Broadly speaking three views were current at the end of the thirteenth century, and their range illustrates very well the complexity of the relationships which were understood to exist between the problem of determining what things are and the problem of saying what they are. Albert the Great had taken the position that existence is an *aliquod*, a something, 'added to essence'. Siger of Brabant took a position at the opposite extreme, that *ens* and *res*, 'being' and 'thing', are words signifying the same essence (*essentia*). He is insistent that they are not merely synonymous. Nor do they signify two 'intentions', as when one says that a man is 'mortal' and 'capable of laughter'. They signify the same intention by different *modus*. *Ens* refers to the *modus* of act; *res* to the *modus* of *habitus*. So the difference in usage of the two terms is merely a matter of *modus significandi*, mode of signifying, and does not imply that something has to be 'added to essence' for a thing to be. A third school of thought regarded *esse* as indeed an addition to the essence of a thing, but in some manner which made it neither an accident nor of the actual essence.[6]

Both the Platonist and the Aristotelian legacy, then, created an atmosphere of heightened awareness about talk of the being or existence of God. That is to say, his existence could not be equated straightforwardly with his being; nor could the available Latin vocabulary for conducting the discussion pass without intimate scrutiny. One solution was to refuse to attempt to talk of God's existence or being at all, or to try to say anything at all about him in a positive way. That approach had a long Christian as well as philosophical history. The Cappadocians, and especially Gregory of Nyssa, had placed an emphasis upon the ultimate inaccessibility of God to human knowing, certainly to the researches of human reason. Ps.-Dionysius takes much the same line, but he goes further. He would argue that incomprehensibility is not a result of the limitation of the human mind only, but a quality of God himself. It follows that we can make no statement which is true of God unless we use negatives. This road leads to mysticism as well as to philosophical consequences, and we find them developing together in a number of Western mediaeval authors, who had some access to this tradition, especially through Eriugena. But it is again instructive to look at Anselm here. In the first chapter of his *Proslogion* he sketches a wholly Western view of the notion of divine inaccessibility. There is no evidence that Anselm knew Pseudo-Dionysian thought, either directly or through Eriugena. Anselm begins by inviting the reader to withdraw into the 'chamber' of his mind, shut out everything but God and close the door. As he prays to God to lead him to himself he is forced to exclaim that God is 'inaccessible', dwelling in 'inaccessible light' (I Timothy 6.16). There is no one who can lead him into that light, and he does not know what signs he should recognise as indicating the presence of God there; he does not know what God 'looks like'. The image of God in Anselm's own person is so damaged and destroyed by sin that it can no longer serve its purpose and show him what God is like. Anselm's resolution of the difficulty is to ask, not to know God as he is, for he knows that that is beyond his understanding, but to seek to know God's 'truth'. That is a truth he already believes and loves, and through his faith he trusts that he may come to some degree of understanding. The thrust of his prayer is not that he may be given an intellectual grasp of trust as a support for faith, but that through faith he may glimpse something of the truth about a God whom he can never wholly understand or know as he is.[7]

Anselm's debt to Augustine is plain enough here, and there are certainly traces of the influence of Platonism which came to him by that route. But he draws directly on the New Testament, too, and he demonstrates the way in which mediaeval scholars could sometimes come more or less independently to theological and philosophical positions which resemble those of predecessors who had in fact not been directly accessible to them.

Anselm's peculiar doctrine of divine knowability is essential to his argument for the existence of God. The notion that nothing can be said of God but what he is not was not necessary to his case. It was, however, central for other mediaeval authors. Late in the twelfth century, Alan of Lille compiled his series of theological axioms, the *Regulae Theologicae*. He was certainly familiar with the Ps.-Dionysian tradition. *Regula* XVIII runs: 'Omnes affirmationes de Deo dicte incompacte, negationes vere.' In his commentary Alan explains that affirmative statements about God differ from affirmative statements about creatures in that when, for example, we say 'Peter is just' we are bringing together 'Peter' and 'justice', so that there is a *compositio*, and we can describe the statement as *compacta*. If we say 'God is just', we make no such link. God's Justice is very God, and the statement is 'incomposite' or *incompacta*. There is no such 'improper' or extraordinary usage or signification when we make a negative statement about God, Alan suggests, because then we are 'removing' from God what is not inherently of his being. He cites Ps.-Dionysius by name as his authority. Alan has adapted the principle that only negative statements can be strictly true of God to the requirements of twelfth-century signification theory, but the core of it is consciously drawn from his source.

With Aquinas we come to a more systematic and developed treatment of the complex of questions on which Anselm, Alan of Lille, Bonaventure and others variously touched. In his *Summa Theologiae* he places the discussion of divine knowability not with the questions about the existence of God and his being, but later, after considering God's simplicity, perfection, goodness, infinity, immutability, eternity and unity. Aquinas argues that it is possible for created intellects to see the essence of God (*ST* I.q.12.a.1), and to do so not by means of a likeness but as he is (a.2). But it is not possible for the created intellect to see God with the bodily eye (a.3) or by its natural powers (a.4). Nor is it possible for creatures to comprehend God (a.7), or to see all that he is, when they see his essence (a.8). Nor can they see his essence at all in this life (aa.11, 12). It seems to Aquinas that God can be named, so long as it is understood that we are naming him only so far as our intellectual powers can know him. That means that in some way or other we must be naming him after created things: as their origin, or by making a comparison which tries to express how much more excellent he is than they. No name which we can predicate of God can express his essence in itself (*ST* I.q.13.a.1). He also disagrees with the school of thought which says that only negative statements can be true of God. He cites arguments based on John of Damascus (*De Fid. Orth.* i.9) and Dionysius (*Div. Nom.* i.4), which support such a view, and dismisses them. He concedes that some negatives are properly affirmed of God, expressing the distance at which his creatures stand from him, or their relation to him. But he himself does not think that affirmative names of God, such as 'good' and 'wise', must properly be read negatively, as expressing some 'remoteness from God' rather than as referring positively to his substance. He mentions Alan of Lille's *Regulae* (21, 26), but only to disagree with him. It is his own opinion that such names signify the divine substance and are predicated substantially of God, although they do not express what he is fully (*ST* I.q.13.a.2).

Meister Eckhart, in the next generation, goes to the opposite extreme from Aquinas' vigorous practicality on the subject of talking positively about God, and takes the mystical experience of a higher awareness as fundamental to any knowledge of God. It was his endeavour to stand, as it were, in the mind of God, so that God-as-other ceases to be the object of the Christian's seeking, and the believer comes to know as God knows, and to be able to say 'My truest "I" is God.' He thought he had thus come to understand that God is not an essence at all, in any sense which human understanding might reach for, as it does when it seeks to know other essences. One can say no more than 'God is', and that is the same thing as to say 'God is not', for God is not this or that. We are led beyond earlier 'negative theology' to a position where we must say nothing is external to God, the awareness of the human knower stands within God, and negative statements about God are necessary only because in human language all affirmations are unavoidably particular and determinate. To affirm something is to exclude what is not affirmed. It is therefore impossible to speak affirmatively of God without implying some restriction or limitation. Only by negations can we gain insight into what God is. So, for example, we may say that he is infinite. That should be seen not as negating any connotation of limit or boundary, but as affirming the negation of limit or boundary, by negating the negative concept of limit or boundary.[8]

With Nicholas of Cusa we come to perhaps the most highly developed, if also the most eccentric, of mediaeval explorations of negative and mystical theology. Nicholas exploited the paradoxes inherent in any such view. For example, in the *De Docta Ignorantia* (I.6ff.) he proves the existence of God defined as Absolute Maximum.[9] One of these must be true: the Absolute Maximum either is or is not; or else it is and is not; or else it neither is nor is not. If one of these must be absolutely true, there exists an Absolute Truth. That must by definition (Nicholas assumes) be identical with the Absolute Maximum. It must also be the case that, since the Absolute Maximum is all that can be, there can be nothing either greater or lesser than that Maximum. But the Minimum is that than which there cannot be a lesser. So we arrive at our paradox, that the Absolute Minimum is identical with the Absolute Maximum. It is also paradoxically true for Nicholas of Cusa that because God is above and prior to all opposing forces, it is in God that all opposites coincide.

The ultimately Neoplatonic traditions on the subject of the being of God, then, weave their threads throughout the mediaeval discussion of divine being, causing no insuperable difficulties to Christian theologians, but making necessary a good deal of stretching of conceptual and linguistic resources.

TRINITY AND DIVINE SIMPLICITY

Christianity inherited the fastidiousness of a philosophical system which cannot countenance the notion of any plurality in God, and regards anything but the utmost simplicity as unworthy of him. That was also a position highly congenial to Islamic monotheism, and Giles of Rome notes that Averroes gives that reason for insisting that there can be no Trinity in God (*Errores Philosophorum* IV.7). But for Christians the doctrine of the Trinity presented a challenge here which had to be taken up.

The particular philosophical difficulties which the doctrine of the Trinity had raised in the first centuries, with the concomitant Christological problems, had not on the whole been causing difficulties in the West since Augustine. Augustine had consolidated an adequate working Latin vocabulary of *substantia* and *persona*, and he had spelt out in his *De Trinitate* the essential principles of the unity of the Godhead and the co-eternity and equality of the Persons which had been so controversial in the early Christian centuries. Boethius had added fresh illustrative material to his account, by way of logical and mathematical analogies. He takes the Pythagorean rule that 'one' can become plural only if some 'otherness' is introduced. (In geometry, for example, any number of points may be piled upon one another and there will still be only one point; but if one point is separated from another along a line, then the points begin to multiply.) The Arians, who tried to establish degrees of merit (*gradus meritorum*) in the Trinity, thus made God a plurality. The equality of the Persons is therefore a guarantee of God's unity, not a source of plurality (*De Trinitate*, 1). In logic we speak of the same and the different in three ways.

Something may be of the same genus (in this way a man is the same as a horse). Father, Son and Holy Spirit are not three Gods but one, because there is no *differentia* to make them differ in species or genus (I). Ten categories can be predicated of everything in creation, but with God everything is of his substance. He is not good but goodness; not merciful but mercy (IV). To predicate substance, quality, quantity of God is to predicate the divine substance, to say what he is (*quid*). The other categories can be reduced to a second 'theological category', that of relation (*ad aliquid*). But in God, the rule of reciprocity which governs ordinary relations does not apply. Where one speaks of a slave one must normally also speak of a master. A father must have a son, and so on. But God the Father was always the Father, and the Son was always the Son. No new relationship came into being with the begetting of the Son, for that is eternal. Sonship and Fatherhood in the Trinity are not interdependent in the same way as they are in creatures (V).

Secondly, we can say that things are of the same species. (Cato is the same as Cicero.) Thirdly, there is also sameness of number. (Tullius is the same person as Cicero.) We can say that things differ numerically. Numerical difference is the result of variety in accidents. Cato and Cicero cannot be in exactly the same place at the same time, but Tullius and Cicero can and must. It is clear that in the Godhead, where there are no accidents, and where genus and species are not applicable either, the rules of logic are challenged, and we are not obliged to speak of many Gods. If 'God' is predicated three times, of Father, Son and Holy Spirit, that does not make three Gods (III).

This treatise of Boethius became the focus of a renewed philosophical debate in the twelfth century. Thierry of Chartres and Gilbert of Poitiers were among those who lectured on his *opuscula* in the schools of northern France before the middle of the century. It was Gilbert who ran into controversy in his attempts to force Latin to encompass ideas it was not yet capable of expressing with technical exactitude. Gilbert tried to explain the relationship between 'God' and his 'divinity', *Deus, divinitas*, by means of an analogy with the natural world, where it is one thing to be and another to be that by which something is: *aliud est quod est, aliud quo est*.[10] Gilbert certainly did not intend to attribute a causative sense to *divinitas* when he spoke of a *Deus a divinitate*;[11] in fact he insisted that *divinitas* is very God.[12] But his opponents suspected him of introducing another God into the discussion, that is, of making God plural. Gilbert was brought to trial at Rheims in 1148 for heresy on this and other counts, but his intricate analysis of the Boethian text continued to be influential among his pupils. (Alan of Lille, much later in the century, included references to Gilbert on Boethius' *De Trinitate* in his *Regulae* (12,12).)

Independently of this formal study of Boethius in the schools, Anselm of Canterbury had returned to the Trinitarian questions at the end of the eleventh century and the beginning of the twelfth, in his treatises on the Incarnation of the Word and the Procession of the Holy Spirit. The first was written during the period when he was moving from Bec to Canterbury, and the second after the Council of Bari in 1098, where Urban II had asked Anselm to construct a case against the Greeks and prove to them that the Spirit proceeds from the Son as well as from the Father. The two treatises are closely related in their concern to establish the simplicity of God in his Trinity. In the first Anselm tries to answer Roscelin of Compiègne, who had been calling him a heretic, and whom Anselm had already striven to silence in an earlier version of the *De Incarnatione Verbi*. Roscelin had cited an example Anselm was evidently fond of using in his talks with his monks. If we say that someone is 'white', 'just', 'literate', we do not mean that he is three separate entities. The force of the analogy is a little different in Latin, because the words *albus, iustus, grammaticus* can serve as nouns as well as adjectives, so that we are also saying 'a white man', 'a just man', 'a literate man'. Roscelin had pressed the image much further than Anselm intended and accused him of saying in effect that either the Trinity was like three souls or three angels; or it must be the case if the Trinity was not thus three *res*, that the Father and the Holy Spirit were incarnate with the Son. This, he claimed, Lanfranc had conceded, and Anselm would agree to if he conducted a disputation with him.[13] Anselm responded by trying to make it clear exactly what he had intended his analogy to do. In suggesting that 'Father', 'Son', 'Spirit' may be said of God in the way 'white', 'just', and so on may be said of a man, he had meant to demonstrate only one or two principles. If the presence or absence of 'fatherhood', 'filiation', 'procession' is said to 'make some change' ('aliquam faciant . . . mutationem') in relation to the divine substance ('circa divinam substantiam'), in the way a man's whiteness or justice can be predicated of him or not; or if it is suggested that the Father[14] can be said to be the Son or the Spirit, Anselm will have nothing to do with such a reading. If his analogy is read as explaining how 'Father', 'Son', 'Holy Spirit' can be predicated of God without making three Gods, he is content. He insists that that is all he said.

Anselm was to discover in his attempt to win over the Greeks to the Western doctrine of double Procession that analogies were dangerously likely to be pressed too far by determined opponents. But this was his first experience of an encounter with a good mind which was determined to outwit him. Roscelin was not silenced. He began again, and this time, Anselm abandoned any attempt to clarify the possibilities of the 'white, just, literate' analogy. He was wise to do so, for he was in fact in deeper waters of speculative grammar than he was technically equipped to swim in.[15] In his second, published letter *On the Incarnation of the Word*, he tackled first the contention that the three Persons must be three things, which would destroy the simplicity of God and make him plural. Anselm presses Roscelin to explain what he means by 'things'. No Christian wants to say that Father and Son are one thing in their Fatherhood and Sonship. But Christians believe that in what is common to them, their Godhead, they are one thing. Again Anselm resorts to the notion of predication, and says that God is unique in that 'Father' and 'Son' are predicated of one Being; if a man is called 'Father', that is in relation to a second man who is his son. So we could certainly say that Father and Son are two things, if that is what we mean by 'thing'. But it is not what Roscelin means. In making the comparison with three angels or three souls, he is slipping from a relational predication (proper uniquely to God) to a substantial predication, which one might use of any created thing (Chapter 2). He is saying that God has three substances and is therefore three Gods. Anselm goes on to develop the implications of Roscelin's error, touching in passing on a notion which may have occurred to him as a result of reading Boethius' *De Trinitate*, if he knew it: that a series of *puncta* is never plural until the points are separated along a line (Chapter 15). Eternity is like that. Instants do not form until there is a difference between them. However often eternity is repeated within itself, it does not become many. Since God is eternity, there can be no plurality of Gods within the Godhead. $1 \times 1 \times 1 = 1$ (Chapter 15).

In the *De Processione Spiritus Sancti*, Anselm examines the ways in which attributes such as eternity, or being Creator, are predicated of God as one, without implying plurality, and asks how it can be that when we say, as we must, that 'Father', 'Son' and 'Holy Spirit' are not all one, but distinct from one another and plural, we do not thereby imply that there is more than one God. It would seem that the unity of God's being makes it impossible to speak of relations within the Trinity; or conversely, that the existence of such relations implies plurality, not unity.

We should look a long way before finding an approach so original, and in some ways so independent of the stock philosophical sources, as that of Anselm. But Peter Abelard, too, tried to think the thing through from first principles. He suggests that the Father, the Son and the Holy Spirit differ not *in essentia* (which would make them three distinct things), but in *status*. Richard of St Victor, a little later, made use of the concept of love between the Persons. In God, he says, there is fullness of love. Perfect love demands plurality, because it must be love of another. In God there is perfect happiness. That requires mutual love. In God there is fullness of glory. True glory is to share generously all one has, and that presupposes an associate in glory. On all these grounds we must postulate Persons in the Godhead, and we can be sure that they are co-eternal, for God is immutable. We can also be sure that they are equal, for mutual love demands equality between lover and beloved.

Some of the devices used in the Boethian *De Trinitate* are adopted and exploited by Alan of Lille in his *Regulae Theologiae*. He stresses that there can be no diversity of parts in God, or plurality of properties, for in God there is nothing but what he himself is. Whatever is in God is God (VIII). Alan seeks to prove as Augustine and Boethius had done, but with some of the additional sophistication of his time, that the divine attributes (as wisdom, holiness, strength) are of God's essence.

Regulae III and IV are concerned with the Trinity. As we saw in Part I, that 'multiplication' of one by one which occurs in the Godhead does not produce multiplicity. Alan describes it as an act of love in which the Father does not cease to be himself, but on his 'other self' (*in se alterum*) the Son, he 'bends' (*reflectit*) that love which is the Holy Spirit. For the Holy Spirit proceeds from the Father in such a way that, by his authority (*eius auctoritate*), he also proceeds from the Son. The use of a principle which allows Alan to insist upon the double Procession of the Holy Spirit is an important development of patristic philosophy in this area, made necessary for him because of the controversy with the Greeks which had separated Eastern and Western Churches since 1054. In *Regula* IV Alan elaborates upon the equality of the Persons of the Trinity. In the Father, he says, is unity *specialiter*; in the Son, *equalitas*, for the Son is the first to be the Father's equal. We may say that there is a *connexio* of unity and equality here.

Alan looks both at general problems of naming God, and at particular questions about predicating the Aristotelian categories of the divine substance. Whenever a term which would refer to a quality if it were used of a creature is predicated of God, it refers to his *essentia* (IX). Although many names may be so predicated, that does not make the divine being plural (IX). That means that when, for example, we call God 'good', we are using the term in a 'copulative' or 'conjunctive' way (*copulata, coniuncta*), because it also implies God's other attributes. ('It is as though I said that God is good, holy, strong', comments Alan.) When I say 'Peter is righteous', that leaves many things outside what is predicated (*extra hanc predicationem*) which apply to Peter, and I must use other terms to predicate those qualities of him (X).

As a prelude to what he has to say about the categories, Alan goes back to *Regula* VIII and derives another rule from it (XI). As a simple being, God's being is one with whatever he is. To say 'God is' is also to say 'God is this and this.' Because there is no diversity or plurality in this being there can be no substance and accident in him, as Boethius maintains when he says (*De Trinitate*, II) that no simple being can be a substance (XII). We may, however, say that God is Form, for he gives form to all things and takes form from none; and we may also say he is Substance, if we understand that this is substance without form, that is, substance without property or accident. Substance understood in this sense is not of the sort to which Boethius objects when he says that no simple being can be a substance (XIII). We may also say that all being is from Form, if God is Form (XIV); because God participated in nothing in order to be, we may say that there is nothing of which his being is (XV); and that his being is formless (*informis*), because the divine Form takes its form from no other (XVI).

Alan pursues these questions of the use of language about God still further. When a noun signifies the divine being, it only seems to signify a quality (*justus*); in the case of God it behaves like a pronoun (*pronominatur*), and signifies not a form attributed to God, but the Divine Form itself (XVII). Similarly, although in other cases we make a 'composite' affirmation when we say, for example, 'Peter is just', in the case of an affirmation made about God, there is nothing 'composite'; while negative statements may be made quite straightforwardly about God (*proprie et vere*) (XVIII). God is just by the justice which is his very self, but when we say he is just, we are really speaking from our knowledge of the effect his justice has on us, and so what he is, is not exactly what he is said to be (XIX). All nouns used of God are used improperly, and so there is propriety in God's being, but impropriety in saying that he is (XX).

Alan agrees with Boethius that to predicate substance, quality, and quantity of God is to predicate the divine substance and to say what he is (*quid*). The other categories can be reduced to a second 'theological category', that of relation (*ad aliquid*) (XXII–XXIII). (Here Alan acknowledges his debt to Augustine, *De Trinitate* V.8.9). But Aquinas asks how we can find a principle upon which there can be understood to be threeness of Persons, when God is immensity, and it would seem that he must embrace all in one. Aquinas uses the mathematical principle that there must be boundaries or limits before there can be plurality. That is to say, 'one' must end before 'two' can begin. In God there is no boundary or limit. But there is a distinction of 'origin' through relation in the Trinity; that is what we understand to be the case in the Persons. There is no boundary or limitation in that, so we can see this distinction as compatible with divine immensity.[16] In the eight Articles of Question 3 of the first part of the *Summa Theologiae*, Aquinas considers simplicity separately from Trinity. He asks whether God is a body, whether he is composed of matter and form, whether he is the same as his own nature, whether being and essence are the same in God, whether God belongs to a genus, has any accidents, is altogether simple, or enters into the composition of other things. In the Questions on the Trinity itself (I q.XXVIIff.), he deals strictly with the implications of the idea of 'relation of origin' (*relatio originis*).

5

THE COSMOS

THE CREATION OF THE WORLD

The question of the eternity of the world

Christians were confronted, just as the ancient philosophers had been, with the problem of explaining how a God of absolute goodness and simplicity could be the Creator of a universe so different from himself, so various and full of multiplicity and corruption; how a God who is eternal and unchanging can have begun at some time to do that which he had not eternally done, and bring the world into being. Christians would point to the Genesis account as a true history of the manner in which the creation took place, but it left a great many philosophical questions unanswered and is unspecific on a good deal of the theology. To take an example: Aquinas asks whether God knows the first instant in which he could have created the world. He answers that there could never have been a time when he could not do so, for his power is eternal and cannot grow or diminish. He says that our task is not, then, to try to settle the instant at which God could have created the world, but the instant at which he did it (*Quodlibet* V.9. q.1.a.1).[1] But that leaves us with the problem that if God created a world which did not exist before he made it, he must have begun at some time to do what he had not eternally done.

If we try to avoid these difficulties we must, it seems, say that God did not create the world. Yet that introduces further problems. We must say either that it exists independently of God, which would argue against his omnipotence; or that it is a part or aspect of God, which is incompatible with his simplicity and immutability, as arguing that he created a world which is temporal and full of differences.

These are difficulties with which the philosophical tradition had grappled too, and it continued to do so. Many of the philosophers of the late antique world were themselves not wholly happy with the options available to them, and especially not with the notion that the world is eternal, if that was taken to mean that the world itself was in some way divine, or part of the divine. The fifth and sixth centuries saw considerable struggles here among Greek-speaking scholars working in the Platonist tradition. A device used by those anxious to refute the views of Aristotle and Proclus on the eternity of the world was to distinguish between a sensible world and an 'intelligible' world, a world of divine ideas which could be regarded as having been always present in the mind of God. Thus the world is eternal only in God's mind. The sensible manifestation of it is not eternal. Aeneas of Gaza, pupil of Hierocles of Alexandria, and founder of the school at Gaza, and his fellow-scholar Zacharias, for example, were among those who wrote on the creation of the world. They agree in seeing the sensible world as a mere appearance by which the eternal, intelligible world is contemplated (*PG* 85.969 and 1021). It is, nevertheless, in some sense a reality, for change and decay may take place in it (*PG* 85.961). The sensible world, with all its characteristics seemingly incompatible with the being of a Neoplatonic God, can thus be seen as not eternal, while the eternity of that which is perfect and immutable in creation is saved by regarding it as part of the 'intelligible' world. But that may be at the cost of regarding God himself as one with this 'intelligible' world.

The Christian Maximus the Confessor (c. 580–662), working within the late Platonist and Pseudo-Dionysian tradition, tried in the next generation to contend that we must regard the 'being' of God as altogether different from the 'being' of the intelligible world. If we do not, he thinks, we are in danger of confusing Creator with creature. He constructs a chain of being to make the difference clear. From the Wisdom of God, he says, come the *logoi*, divine powers or wills, principles of existence eternally existing in the divine Mind. They bring into being the 'intelligibles' which, once they have come into existence, cannot cease to exist. But whereas the *logoi* are really one, the intelligibles are many (*PG* 91.1329; 1081; 1085). The thrust of his argument is the reverse of that of Aeneas and Zacharias of Gaza, who wanted to use the concept of the 'intelligible world' as a means of reconciling the eternity of the world with its corruptibility on the one hand and with the Neoplatonic rules about the nature of God on the other. Maximus seeks to show that the intelligible world is definitely neither God himself nor in some way co-eternal with him as present always in his mind.

In the mediaeval period the question of the eternity of the world did not again become an urgent philosophical issue until the thirteenth century, with the rediscovery of Aristotelian natural science. Among the 'errors of the philosophers' condemned by Giles of Rome were several touching on this point. He said, for example, that Aristotle teaches that the sublunary world was being generated from eternity and will never cease (I.6). Averroes offends by reasserting with more force still all Aristotle's errors about the eternity of the world (IV). Aquinas was prepared to go so far as to say that the world is eternal as an idea in the mind of God (*Quod*. IV. q.1.a.1, p. 71). But he cannot accept that the world itself is eternal. On the other hand, he cannot demonstrate that it is not. He says it must remain a matter of faith (*Quod*. XII.q.6.a.1). The matter became a standard issue of conflict between the philosophical tradition and Christian orthodoxy in the 1260s and 1270s at Paris, and beyond.[2]

The boundary between Creator and creation

The sixth-century Christian and philosophical reaction against Proclus in the Greek-speaking world included John Philoponus (c. 475–565). This philosopher who became a Christian approached the problem in a rather different way. He sought to determine exactly where the 'boundary' was to be drawn between the stuff which may be deemed divine and eternal, and the stuff we call matter. An indispensable preliminary here is to agree on which side of the line the stars, sun and moon fall. Philoponus' approach was to prove helpful to the Christian scholars of the West (for whom Aristotle was to be a more direct influence than Proclus, the questions of natural science increasingly urgent, and the Pseudo-Dionysian tradition always an awkward bedfellow). Philoponus drew his boundary of demarcation in such a way that the stars and planets are included with everything on earth in the category of mutable matter; he did so with a convincingness which was to provide a secure basis for Christian doctrine on this point thereafter.[3] If we think in this way of an eternal God, and a world made of matter which is not eternal, we have a position incompatible with either Aristotle or Proclus.

But it did not immediately resolve the problem (which arises partly out of a failure to distinguish physics from metaphysics) of the incommensurability between an eternal, changeless, omnipotent and perfectly good God and a world which is none of these things, although he is its Creator. The problem is put in simple terms by Alcuin (c. 735–804) in the Carolingian West. He cites the fourth-century Marius Victorinus (who became a Christian in old age) on the paradox that God is one and alone, even though he wanted there to be many things. Alcuin explores the implications of saying that God makes his creatures without lending them part of his own substance. (For he did not want them to be as he was, Alcuin says: 'illud esse . . . quod ille ipse est'.)[4]

By the end of the Middle Ages the problem of incommensurability looked much more complicated. In the *De Docta Ignorantia* Nicholas of Cusa tried to explain the paradox by saying that there can be no proportionality between the finite and the infinite. Always lurking temptingly in the background was the hypothesis that God effects a 'join' between himself and the world by entering it as its soul. There was a very considerable body of philosophical literature available to the Latin West, in addition to Plato's *Timaeus*, which postulated a world-soul (and Calcidius' commentary on the point). Virgil speaks of it in the sixth book of the *Aeneid* (VI.726–7) as diffused throughout the world's 'body', a 'mind' which moves inert matter. Cicero, in *The Dream of Scipio*, and Macrobius in his commentary on the *Dream* were important too. Macrobius describes the *anima mundi* as imparting perpetual motion to the body of the heavens which it has created (*In Somn. Scip.* I.17, pp. 541–2).

There was Christian warrant for the idea in Genesis and in Acts (17.25ff.). But Augustine was aware that a major question arises here about the difference between a ubiquitous Holy Spirit, who is present in the world but is God, not creature, and who is not himself the world; and the notion of the pagan philosophers that the world-soul is a supernatural power inherent in the phenomenal world and sustaining it as its life.

The fine but crucial difference was puzzled over by the mediaeval generations. In his twelfth-century *Philosophia*, William of Conches explores the possibility that the world-soul is indeed the Holy Spirit, for it is by the Holy Spirit that all things live. Or it may be a 'natural vigour' which God puts into things. Or it may be an incorporeal substance which is wholly present in each individual body (*PL* 172.46). Thierry of Chartres touches on the problem (*TC*, p. 273). Arnald of Bonneval tries to define the world-soul in a way which makes it the overflowing abundance of the Holy Spirit who gives all things, rational and irrational, what they need for their being (*PL* 189.1673). Bernardus Silvestris tries a poetical solution. He writes of the marriage of the soul of the world and the world, which results in the organisation of the four elements in an orderly way and the resolution of chaos into harmony. This is betokened by the descent of the world-soul (*endelichia*) from the heavens in a chorus of mathematical and musical harmonies. But Bernardus Silvestris is deliberately vague about the exact origin and identity of the world-soul and its relation to Nous. Nous serves merely as the priest who performs the ceremony.[5]

The problem was still in play after the arrival of Aristotle's *Libri naturales*. David of Dinant, one of the first to read the *Physics*, *Metaphysics* and *De Anima*, drew from his proof that God is the material cause of all things (*principium materiale omnium*) the conclusion that God himself is 'the one sole substance, not only of all bodies but also of all souls . . . and Plato and Xenophon the philosophers agree; they say the world is nothing but God perceptible to us'.[6] David of Dinant's views were condemned, but it is instructive that the impact of the new Aristotle should so quickly have been to throw orthodoxy a little off course in the mind of at least one Christian scholar.

It cannot be said that Western philosophy or theology arrived at a wholly satisfactory solution of all these problems. God was understood to be separate from and other than the world. The world was agreed not to be eternal. But deep questions remain.

Creation from nothing

Plato says in the *Timaeus* that God worked with pre-existing matter and form to create the world. This was a view unacceptable to Augustine, who had dealt firmly with the question, and insisted that God had made the world from nothing. That became the standard Christian position for Western scholars.

For Thierry of Chartres, it is necessary only to insist that God needed nothing when he created the world; his supreme goodness and absolute sufficiency were enough. He made the world out of kindness and love, and for no other reason, so that there might be beings to share his happiness (TC, pp. 555–6). There is no difficulty in Thierry's mind about the status of the stuff of which the world was made. God created it at the first instant (p. 557). Thierry does not find it necessary to seek to explain how the eternal and immutable God could have brought into being a world so evidently his inferior. Hugh of Amiens, Thierry's contemporary, similarly unworried by the central concern of Neoplatonism, puts the matter straightforwardly. 'If perhaps you were to look for something before the creation of things, you would not be able to find anything at all. Only eternity was there before all things, only God . . . The changeableness of the creature proves that it had a beginning.' Those men of old who trusted to the proofs of their own senses and said that God, matter and form were co-eternal and God no more than a craftsman were judging by human standards (*tamquam de se*). They thought God could do no more than they themselves could do. Like Thierry, he explains that God did not create the world in any need of his own, or out of any need of his own, but 'through towering charity' (*per caritatem supereminentem*).

The mode of creation

In Genesis creation takes place as God speaks. That was not wholly impossible to reconcile with Platonic and Neoplatonic theories about the work of the *Logos*, although it presented early Christian thinkers with a number of difficulties. But more important for the Middle Ages was a model, or group of models, of creation which have in common some notion of divine overflowing, propagation or multiplication. The idea of an emanation in which God pours himself out upon creation, himself undiminished by his giving, but bringing the created world into being as he does so is clearly present in Augustine: 'cum effunderis super nos, non tu dissiparis, sed colligis nos' (*Conf.* I.3). In this spatial world, God is wholly everywhere and yet he is in no place (Augustine, *Conf.* VI.3). This is an image which Alan of Lille makes use of in a form attractive to other mediaeval writers. God is a sphere, he says, whose centre is everywhere and whose circumference is nowhere (*Regulae Theologiae*, VII). A sphere has no beginning or end; God is a sphere, not to the bodily eye, but to the eye of the understanding; but he is a sphere unlike any other, for in a bodily sphere the centre is a point which has no dimension, and therefore no place, and the circumference is in a multitude of places. In the divine sphere of creation, the centre is the creature, a tiny point in comparison with the immensity of God, and having a fixed place; the immensity of God is the circumference, and in him there is no *locus*.[7]

Cognate with this picture of the paradox of an emanation which brings into being something other than God, and which does not take from God in doing so anything of what he is (although it takes its being and nature wholly from him), is the image of creation as an act of divine illumination.[8] This, too, is a strong Augustinian theme, although Augustine is especially interested in the notion of that part of the creative act which is an illumination of the understanding.[9] Divine illumination as creative act is an important theme in Robert Grosseteste, who also links it closely with the doctrine that the mind needs spiritual illumination in order to comprehend God and the universe he has made.[10]

Arabic philosophers took up the theme of emanation from the Greeks, and their influence was significant in bringing Latin scholars (from the twelfth century) to make use of it too.[11]

In Nicholas of Cusa's hands the paradoxes multiply. He sees the universe as unfolded from God, and yet as in some sense a 'restricted' or 'contracted' 'maximum'. God is the absolute 'whatness' (*quidditas*) of the created world, but the created world is a 'contracted quiddity' (*quidditas contracta*) because it is finite, and every created thing is itself a contradiction even of that, just as every species is a contraction of a genus. So the overflowing of divine abundance in the generosity of creation results in a series of ever tighter contractions.[12] Here, too, it is possible to see a connection with familiar ideas of the Platonic tradition. Augustine points out that as created things are further from God in the stream of outpouring, so they become less and less like him (*De Civ. Dei* IX.17).[13]

From Pythagorean mathematics came yet another variant of the idea of creation by emanation. Nicomachus of Gerasa wrote an *Arithmetica* in the Pythagorean tradition upon which Boethius' *Arithmetica* is heavily dependent. The underlying theory of numbers is that all proceeds from one. One is itself not a number but the source of numbers, which it produces by means of plurality. Plurality is dependent upon the presence of some 'otherness'. The idea was familiar to Anselm, as we have seen in his treatment of the Trinity (see p. 60ff.). Alan of Lille develops it in discussing both Trinity and creation. He begins his sequence of *Regulae* from the principle that God is not only One, but that unity from which all plurality, all diversity proceeds. Unity itself is without resource, and it is itself the source of all plurality without itself becoming plural. Moreover, when one is multiplied by one, no plurality is generated; so it is that the Father begets the Son and the Holy Spirit proceeds from the Father while God remains one (pp. 124–5). The concepts here are those of Pythagorean mathematics, again mediated through Boethius, especially in his *De Arithmetica*, with an admixture of elements Alan is likely to have taken from the work of his own contemporaries.[14]

He follows the same line of thought in *Regula* II in saying that God is unity above the heavens; the angelic creation that *alteritas* or 'secondness' which is not truly plural but is the first departure from unity; beneath the heavens lies all plurality, in those bodily things whose multiplicity and variety are *obnoxia*. Here a further notion is crucial: that variety and difference, which do not resemble God, are necessarily evil. Again it is an idea with a long post-Platonic history.

Roger Bacon tried to apply the mathematical idea of multiplication and the principles of the behaviour of light to the question of the multiplication of species. He envisaged a power specific to each kind of being propagated from its ultimate divine source in all directions, like rays of light, through material suitable for forming the appropriate species. Because all materials or media must offer some resistance to the passage of the rays of 'species', there will inevitably be some weakening of the ray as species multiply. Eventually the multiplication will come to an end.

Alongside the development of these essentially Platonic principles ran theories of causation, which had vigorous Aristotelian roots although they are also to be found in the Neoplatonic writers. (Proclus, for example, argues that all producing causes produce secondary existences because they have a superfluity of power, while not themselves being changed or diminished; and that the effect will resemble the cause).[15] Aristotle himself argues in the *Metaphysics* (994ᵃ) against the possibility that there can be an infinite chain of causes. Certain principles passed into Western thinking much in the form in which they are set out by Proclus in his *Elements of Theology*. It is taken as axiomatic that the cause is superior to the effect in the hierarchy of being. The final cause is God himself. This final cause is identical with the Good, and it is One. It is, however, also identical with the efficient cause which actually brings created things into being. Both the final and the efficient causes are transcendent, and yet paradoxically able to act upon a world which is other than they (*Propositions* 7–13).

The notion of the four causes (final, efficient, formal and material), was familiar in the West before the introduction of the full Aristotelian corpus. It is described, for example, by Seneca (*Epistulae Morales* LXV). Thierry of Chartres identifies the efficient cause with God, the formal cause with the Wisdom of God, the final cause with his Kindness (*benignitas*), and the material with the four elements, which are themselves God's creation (TC, p. 555).[16] We also find in Thierry a distinction between first and secondary causes. God is the first cause and first principle of all things (TC, p. 174.83), but there is a series of causes in an orderly *conexio* (*sic*) in the creation of the world (TC, p. 273.28–32).

Aquinas tackles awkward questions about causation in the *Summa Theologiae*. It is argued that God cannot himself be the exemplary cause of all things because the effect must resemble the cause, and creatures do not resemble God (*ST* I.q.45.a.3, Obj. 1). They do, however, resemble the ideas in the mind of God on which they are formed, replies Aquinas. If it is suggested that God cannot be the final cause of all things because that would seem to imply that he has need of a purpose (*ST* I.q.45.a.4, Obj. 1), or because that would make him both efficient and final cause, both before and after, which is impossible (*ibid.*, Obj. 4), Aquinas has answers. God is unique among agents in that he acts from no need of his own. He is not only the final and efficient but also the exemplary or formal cause of all things; all that means is that the first principle of all things is ultimately one. There is no dispute over the usefulness or the validity of the adoption of Aristotelian thinking about causation in the context of a Christian doctrine of creation. The debate is solely about the precise manner in which it may be made to fit.

Like Thierry, Aquinas speaks of primary and secondary causes. For example, in discussing the way in which human free will acts in accordance with predestination, he argues that there is no distinction between the two. Divine providence produces effects as first cause through the operation of secondary causes. So we may say that what is done by choice (secondary cause) is also predestined (*ST* I.q.23.a.5).

Thomas Bradwardine was the author of a 'victory sermon', preached after the battle won at Crécy on 26 August 1346. In it he explores theories of causation erroneously held by astrologers, those who believe in fortune; those who believe in the fates; those who trust to human prowess or the wisdom of human advice, or even to virility or sexual prowess. Only God is the author of victory, he says, as he is the cause of all things.[17]

SUSTAINING THE WORLD

The Creator's work is not deemed by philosophers or by Christian theologians to be finished when he has made the world. He sustains it in being. Divine work here is discussed on two levels in both traditions. The first is that of the divine plan for the world, with all the concomitant questions about providence, divine omnipotence, and the problem of evil, together with the issues of divine foreknowledge, predestination, grace and the free will of rational creatures. Here we must get ahead of ourselves a little and consider the problem of free will before we come to the philosophy and theology of 'man' (see p. 90ff.). The second level is that of what today we might call natural science, that is, the considerations which affect the mechanical running of things.

Divine omnipotence

Are there things God cannot do? In the late thirteenth-century crisis, questions challenging the power of God at particular points were popular among 'philosophers', and they presented theologians with substantial difficulties. Some were already familiar: Can God restore lost virginity?[18] Can God cause a body to be present in two places? (This last had special urgency because of the implications of the doctrine of transubstantiation. Giles of Rome makes a familiar distinction, that the body of Christ is *localiter* in heaven, *sacramentaliter* present on innumerable altars.)[19] Some were designed to place the theologian in a position where he must either deny a truth he wishes to predicate of God or deny his omnipotence. Can God sin if he wishes? Can God cause two contradictories to be simultaneously true? (The condemnation of the 219 Articles in 1277 said not.)[20]

The problem of evil

Such games-playing with paradoxes had a more serious aspect. These questions struck at fundamentals of the whole Christian system. The root difficulties all came back in the end to the problem that it is not easy to understand how a God who is perfectly good and all-powerful can possess both these attributes when there is evil in the world. If he can be shown to be a being of modified power or assailable goodness, the problem is soluble; but then we are left with a God who is less than all that both the Platonic and the Christian traditions had claimed for him. The attempt to avoid having to regard God as the author of evil had generated the Gnostic and Manichee dualist traditions. These continued in the Middle Ages among Cathars, Bogomils and Albigensians, heresies of great popularity from the twelfth century in certain parts of Europe.[21]

Almost all Christian authors of the mediaeval period followed the common philosophical view of the ancient world that evil is nothing, an absence of the good. It was worked out fully in the Latin tradition by Augustine, and no mediaeval author made a serious attempt to produce an alternative hypothesis. There were, however, mediaeval refinements. Anselm asks, as Augustine had done, how 'nothing' can be so devastating in its effect. He explores the notion that the absence of what ought to be has a certain positive force, because the 'ought' imposes an imperative. He also takes up and develops considerably further the problem addressed by Augustine in the *De Magistro*, and later by the Carolingian scholar Fredegisus, that (since every word signifies something) the word 'evil', like the word 'nothing', signifies something, or it would not be a word at all. Anselm suggests that the word 'evil', like the word 'nothing', signifies the removal of a something which must itself be signified together with the concept of its absence. It signifies not (in the usual way) by establishing the something, but by removing it. He points out that there are many examples of the use of words in similar ways, where the form of the expression does not coincide with the fact. To say that someone is blind is not really to say that he has blindness, but that he lacks sight. When we say 'Evil caused this', we are speaking as though evil were a something, or, as Anselm prefers to put it, a 'sort-of-something' ('quasi-aliquid'). Here we see even the relatively elementary language-theory of Anselm's period, which depends upon the *logica vetus* and the Roman grammarians, being put to philosophically sophisticated use (*De Casu Diaboli*, 11). The 'defect' theory of evil was also used by mediaeval authors (in a manner pioneered by Anselm) to explain how there can be things an omnipotent God cannot do. Aquinas, for example, says that if God cannot do what is repugnant to his being, there is no defect of divine power (*Quod*. III.q.a.1).

Some aspects of the problem of evil overlap with the question of providence. Augustine again gave a lead here, especially in *The City of God*, where he confronts the problem of explaining why God should allow the fall of a Christian Roman Empire if he is indeed omnipotent. He presents a case for the view that God's providential plan is so far beyond our grasp in its immensity and benevolence that we have simply got the matter out of scale. Boethius added substantially to the literature in the *De Consolatione Philosophiae*, which had a great influence in the Middle Ages. There he investigates not only providence, but chance, fate and fortune, in connection with the question of divine foreknowledge, predestination and the role of human free will. To the man who does not understand God's providential plan, fortune seems fickle and malevolent, ingratiating herself, and just when she is trusted, deserting the unfortunate (*Cons*. II, pr.1). To the believer it becomes clear that all fortune, good or bad, is under God's control, and rewards or punishes. It is therefore profitable, and in that sense a good, even if it is in another sense bad fortune (IV, pr.vii). Divine providence, says Boethius, is the very reason of God; it disposes all created things and brings them to their due end. Providence places all individual created things a disposition to act in a certain way which we call fate. But that is within providence and under its control (IV, pr.vi). This line of argument satisfied Peter Abelard, who is prepared to go so far as to say that if there is evil in the universe, it must be there within God's divine providential plan. It must therefore be good that there is evil (Thomas, pp. 162–3). That can be allowed only with many provisos, as earlier authors had realised. The Carolingian debate about the theory of double predestination turned on precisely this point, for if God predestines some to hell, it seems he must be the author of hell. The late eleventh and twelfth centuries saw considerable discussion on questions of God's 'permission' of evil.

A further paradox familiar to ancient philosophy troubled the mediaeval world. If all falling away from the good is evil, and all created things depart in their natures in varying degrees from the Creator, must we conclude that the created world is evil? The Gnostic tradition was inclined to think so, at least in so far as it is the case that the created world is also in large measure the material world. Again, it would seem either that a creator God must be the author of evil, or that he must be less than omnipotent, if we save him from that consequence by postulating the independent existence *ab eterno* of the matter which taints his world.

The framework in which philosophers and Christians alike were inclined to set all this was that of a universe which not only streams out of God but is also perpetually trying to return to him. Returning to God, his creatures enter into his likeness. Falling away from God they enter the 'region of unlikeness' (Plato, *Politics* 273^d). Genesis 1.26 seemed to confirm this for Christians with its reference to man's being made in God's image and likeness. Augustine speaks of the *regio dissimilitudinis* in his *Confessions* and seems to refer to it elsewhere. Bernard of Clairvaux took the image up in the twelfth century, probably drawing on Augustine, but perhaps also upon Plato and Athanasius and others who make use of it in various forms. There is a possibility of some borrowing from Plotinus too.[22]

Future contingents and divine foreknowledge

Propositions about the future present a difficulty which does not occur in the case of statements about the present or the past, as Aristotle pointed out in the *De Interpretatione* (IX). Propositions are either true or false. Therefore every predicate must belong to its subject or not. If someone says that a particular event will happen and another says that it will not, only one can be speaking the truth. Otherwise two incompatible predicates would both belong to one subject. But if it is true now either that something will take place or that it will not, it would seem that nothing can be contingent, that all events must come about of necessity (18^{a-b}).

Aristotle's problem does not directly involve the notion of foreknowledge. It is about the puzzle of the truth or falsehood of statements made in the present about a future which is hidden from the speaker. Nor does he introduce an omniscient and foreseeing divine eye, with all the concomitant complications of having to allow for the fact that such a being can never be in error about the future, if he is also omnipotent. Boethius, whose work on the *De Interpretatione* was of the first importance in bringing the problem of future contingents before early mediaeval minds, extended the question in these directions in his *Consolation of Philosophy*. If it is true that someone is sitting, we understand that he is not 'sitting because it is true that he is sitting'; on the contrary, it is true that he is sitting only because he is in fact sitting. Boethius reasons that the same must apply to future events. They do not happen because they are foreseen. On the other hand, it cannot be the case that God's prescience is at the mercy of what-is-going-to-happen, so that the happening governs the operation of his providence (V, pr.3). There is the further problem of the manner in which God can foreknow things which may occur but will not necessarily occur. If he foreknows them and they do not occur, he will be mistaken, and it is impious to think that even possible. But if he foreknows that they 'either will or will not happen', that cannot be called foreknowledge at all, for he would be 'knowing' an uncertainty (*ibid.*).

Building on these texts, Anselm of Canterbury was able to take things a little further. He realised that questions not only of formal predication but also of usage were involved in framing propositions about necessity. We often say something 'must be' when no compelling force is involved. ('God must be immortal.') 'It is necessary that you will choose to sin' is a statement of this sort. We need not postulate compulsion. To say 'If God foreknows this, it will therefore necessarily happen' is to say more than 'If this thing will happen, it will necessarily happen.' It is a tautology, not a statement about cause and effect (*De Concordia* I.2).[23] Alan of Lille did not think the problem about causation could be avoided in this way.[24] He tried to answer the question 'whether the foreknowledge of God is the cause of what is to happen'. Since whatever God foreknows must come about, it would seem that in the case of God prescience implies necessity and is actually the cause of the future. Conversely, if something was not to happen, God would know that it was not to happen. On the other hand, he recognises that if divine foreknowledge is seen as causative in a perfectly straightforward way, there is no escaping the conclusion that God is the author of evil. A century later, Giles of Rome confronts questions raised in the sometimes half mischievous spirit of the late thirteenth-century debates with the *philosophi* of the Arts Faculties. Do angels know future contingents? (The wicked angels present interesting difficulties here, and the case of Merlin is cited, for he is said to have been born with a demon's aid, and he knew the future, as it were, standing on its head.) Giles's view is that angels can have nothing in their minds but what really exists; future contingents have an indeterminant existence; therefore angels cannot have certain knowledge of them (*Quodlibet* X, p. 21). Nevertheless, since angelic knowledge is not limited by time in the manner of human knowledge, the question is wickedly clever, and raises new difficulties. For Bradwardine in the fourteenth century the crux of the matter is the paradox that whatever God does must be perfectly free, and yet everything God does could not be done in any other way because it is done in the best possible way; and so it would seem that whatever God does is necessary.[25]

Free will, predestination and grace

The question of future contingents and divine foreknowledge cannot be discussed for long by Christian theologians without its becoming entangled with that of free will, predestination and the operation of grace. The philosophical heritage here was mixed. The Stoics tended to think all actions determined, though some stress that it is an exercise of freedom to accept the inevitable willingly. Thinkers who regarded the stars as indicators and predictors of future events were also determinists. But Carneades led a Platonist revolt against a hard determinist line by arguing that if men are but puppets, there can be no ground for praise or blame and no justice in reward or punishment.

Augustine described the way in which one topic leads into the other in his *City of God*. In Cicero's *De Divinatione*, he says, it is denied that there can be any knowledge of future things in God or man. On the other hand, in writing *On the Nature of the Gods*, Cicero seems to Augustine to be covertly defending the opposite view. He puts Cicero's difficulty down to an unwillingness to deny the existence of free will, on the grounds that once one allows that the future can be known, one must concede the existence of fate, and Cicero was afraid of the implications that doctrine must have for freedom of choice (*De Div. Dei* V.9). The same consequence was apparent to Boethius, who also traces the link between divine foreknowledge and the destruction of free will in man

(*Cons*, V, pr.3), and points out that men will then be condemned for acts to which they have been driven by necessity; prayer will be pointless, for it cannot avert anything which is to come (*ibid.*).

Augustine wrestled with the relationship of divine foreknowledge; human free will; predestination; and the peculiarly Christian concept of a divine grace (which is personal, merciful and enabling in a way that the pagan 'fate' was not) throughout the decades in which he was writing against the Pelagians.[26] Towards the end of his life he became more and more convinced that God predestines those he will save and that human free will was maimed by the Fall in such a way that while we can of ourselves continue to will evil, we cannot will good without the direct intervention of God in the form of the action of grace.

The issue was taken up again controversially in the ninth century by Godescalc of Orbais. He contended that if God foreordains some to good, he must also determine the destiny of those who are to go to hell. Augustine had stopped short of this doctrine of double predestination, because it seemed to him that it would make God the author of evil. By teaching that our wrong actions are our own fault, while our good actions are made possible only by grace, Augustine left the fault of the wicked with themselves. Godescalc's position was attacked by Eriugena in his *De Divina Praedestinatione*[27] on the grounds that neither divine prescience nor predestination by God compels. Our sins are our own fault. Free choice is a good gift of God, even though it can be misused (V–VII). He gives a good deal of space at the end of his treatise to the texts of Scripture which seem to suggest that God foreknows or predestines sin or death. Eriugena draws on the rhetorical tradition – in a way Augustine encouraged in the *De Doctrina Christiana* – to show that statements can sometimes be intended to be understood to say the opposite of what they seem to say (IX–X ff.). Eriugena is left with the tasks of explaining how man can bring about his own downfall for himself without that implying a defect of divine omnipotence; and how we are to account for the existence of hell if God is not responsible for it.

In dealing with the first, he depends on Augustine's view that sin and evil are negations. When the sinner does wrong he casts himself upon nothing. God is not the author of nothing. In exploring the notion of hell he owes a conspicuous debt to cosmic notions drawn from the philosophical tradition. There was already a movement afoot to try to locate a place of punishment in the universe. Eriugena prefers a Miltonic theory that the mind is its own place and creates in itself its place of torment. Both the blessed and the damned dwell in the life to come in the high places of the cosmos where the element of fire is to be found.

But whereas for the blessed that life is a place of brightness and beauty, for the wicked it is a region of infinite pain (*PL* 122.436ff.). There is undoubtedly an Augustinian influence here too, from the *De Ordine* perhaps, where the beauty of order is seen as involving some *chiaroscuro*.

When we come to Anselm, we find a different complexion put upon the philosophical considerations. Anselm starts from Augustine's assumptions that sin and evil are nothing, but he achieves a more subtle balance than any of his predecessors in trying to account for the coexistence of the freedom of choice of rational beings with divine foreknowledge, predestination and grace. He wrote on freedom of choice in the series of little treatises which he put together for the monks of Bec soon after writing the *Monologion*. It seems to him that the crux of the matter is the meaning of 'freedom'. Neither God himself nor the good angels are able to sin, and yet we must call them free. Freedom must be the same for man, too. Therefore 'to be able to sin' cannot be a part of freedom (*De Lib. Arb.* 1). His pupil in the dialogue objects that he cannot see why a being which has the power both to sin and not to sin is not more free than one who cannot sin. Anselm encourages him to take the view that the being which cannot sin actually possesses what is beneficial and appropriate (that is, the freedom to do good) in a higher degree than one who can lose what he possesses (*ibid.*). Anselm goes on to show that freedom of choice is best defined as the ability to keep *rectitudo* or rightness of will purely for its own sake. God has this freedom of himself; rational creatures who are among God's elect have it of him.

Much later, near the end of his life, Anselm returned to the theme, and wrote a *De Concordia* in which he set out to demonstrate the harmony of freedom of choice with divine foreknowledge, predestination and grace. He begins by contrasting the necessary futurity of things foreknown by God with the contingent futurity of what is done by free choice. If these are incompatible, then freedom of choice cannot coexist with divine foreknowledge. He shows that, on the contrary, there is no clear-cut opposition between the two. It is possible to distinguish between what must necessarily occur in the future (the sun will rise tomorrow) and what will in fact occur, although it is possible that it will not (tomorrow there will be rebellion among the people) (I.3). Moreover, not all that will necessarily occur involves an element of compulsion. It is necessary for God to be immortal, but he is not under compulsion so to be (I.2). For a thing to be future is not the same as for a future thing to be future (I.2). In these and other ways he opens up the Boethius–Aristotle discussion of future contingents. He argues that although all the actions of the will are themselves caused by God, for actions have being and God is the source of all being, the willing of good men and good angels is perfectly free because it is the supreme beauty of their freedom that they will to choose the good; their wills must therefore be in harmony with what God wills, and so his actions are freely theirs. Similarly, the evil wills of the fallen freely turn away from God's will, and it is that which makes their actions evil; the actions themselves are not evil, because God is their author (I.7). Thus we may say that divine foreknowledge of what is to be is compatible with human and angelic freedom of choice.

But arguments from absence of compulsion in necessity cannot so easily meet the case of the relationship between predestination and freedom of choice. And certainly God's foreknowledge must coincide with his predestination. But this gives Anselm a means of getting round the difficulty. God foreknows only what will occur, either freely or necessarily. And so he predestines only what will occur in the same way. He meets Godescalc's point about the apparent inevitability of double predestination (and encompasses the Scriptural passages which seem to imply it) by explaining that an improper usage is involved when God is said to cause evils (II.2, 3). Grace is seen as aiding the free choice of the good in many ways (III.1). It is only ever withheld when the will by free choice abandons the rightness (*rectitudo*) it has been given, and wills something it should not. So grace is available to all but those who reject it. God can thus justly condemn those who do not have his grace.

In the Anselmian account the Augustinian parameters are respected. Anselm, like Augustine, accepts predestination of the elect. But he achieves a philosophically more sophisticated and in many ways original statement of the relationship of freedom of choice to the foresight and predestination which must be attributed to an omniscient and omnipotent God.

With the arrival of the *Nicomachean Ethics* of Aristotle in the West in the century after Anselm there was a substantial addition to the available philosophical literature on free will. Aristotle's view is that human will tends towards what is for human good. Right choice is the result of making a judgement about what is for one's good in particular circumstances. The right choice will therefore differ from one individual to another and from circumstance to circumstance (*Ethics* 1112^a). This notion that free choice-making is at the disposal of reason acting upon the evidence had its influence on Christian theologies. William of Auxerre, for example, stresses the practicality and rationality of good choices; and a number of other thirteenth-century authors, Hugh of St

Cher and Richard Fishacre, for instance, reflected upon the role of reason in relation to the will.[28] This stress on the rational will needed reconciling with Augustine's teaching that human will is damaged by the Fall so that it can no longer do good without the aid of grace, and reason is likewise damaged so that it cannot reason aright.

The classic issues were still current. Aquinas finds himself discussing in a *Quodlibet* whether predestination imposes a necessity (*Quod.* XI.q.3.a.1). He distinguishes necessary (divine) and contingent (human voluntary) causation in predestination, in ways earlier authors were able to do, but it comes naturally to his mind to speak of predestination in an Aristotelian and teleological way as *directio in finem*. He was well aware of the complexity of the problems this 'most famous question' raises, and his own thinking altered during the course of his career. In the *De Veritate* he describes free choice as an act of judgement by reason; he tries in this way to establish the superiority of reason in determining the actions of the will. John Quidort, Godfrey of Fontaines and others supported his theory that the will must concur with what reason tells it is for the best. But among the Franciscans some (for example, Alexander of Hales) held that freedom of choice directed both will and reason; others (as Bonaventure) preferred to see freedom of choice as a *habitus*, not a power or faculty of the soul. John of La Rochelle rolled all three together into a single faculty of reason and will and choice-making.[29]

This debate bore controversial fruit in the fourteenth century in the outbreak of a new 'Pelagian' controversy. The advocates of the 'Pelagian' view argued that it must either be the case that God looks away so that human actions may be freely entered into without his foreseeing them (which places a restriction on his omnipotence), or it must happen that he foresees but permits what he knows to be contingent, not necessary. This last possibility would allow for the eventuality that God's plan for the world, providence itself, even the scheme of revelation, might have been or might be different. In response Bradwardine wrote his *De Causa Dei*, an ambitious work designed to fit the whole debate into the scheme of a full systematic theology of divine being and creation. God, says Bradwardine, knows everything specifically, and his knowledge is complete. It is also eternal and immutable, and he knows past, present and future alike. Everything which God knows is actively moved by him. His knowledge is therefore an active force. Nothing can happen unless God wills it. Even what he 'permits' is his act. To the question, how then can God not be held responsible for sin, Bradwardine replies that sin comes from the wills of men and evil angels alone, but that God must be regarded as in some sense its 'negative cause'. He uses it as a means of punishing where punishment is deserved and as a source of pattern and order in the universe (for the good is more beautiful when we can see its opposite).

All this rests upon an Ockhamist doctrine of divine absolute power. For Ockham nothing was impossible to God; God can in principle do even that which seems to go against his very nature. His *potentia absoluta* can even override his *potentia ordinata*, that is, the power by which he enacts particular things in the created world. Aquinas, too, had argued the point. In a *Quodlibet* on whether God can make something return to nothing, he distinguishes between God's absolute power (by which he can certainly do so), and his power acting within the order prescribed by his wisdom and foreknowledge (by which he does not do so) (*Quod.* IV.q.3.a.1). This distinction has a long mediaeval history. It was already clear to Anselm. The key question was whether a God who is as Christians believe him to be will ever do that which goes against his nature, and whether, as Anselm would put it, to do what ought not to be done is in fact an act of impotence rather than one of power.

The running of the world

Ancient philosophical thought sought to explain how the natural world runs, in terms of causes both physical and metaphysical. Interference could be postulated, from ill-disposed or well-intentioned spiritual powers, but that brought the question into the realms of the magical arts. These lay on the fringes of the intellectually respectable in philosophy, as they lay on the edge of the orthodox in Christian thought of the Middle Ages. The overall purpose of the philosophers was to account for nature and its phenomena in terms of a co-ordinated system of forces and tendencies, moving matter according to regulating principles derived from a higher power. Christian thought introduced a new element into the equation in the form of grace. Grace is the free act of a merciful God. It can alter the course of otherwise predictable events for good.

Grace's primary action is in connection with the will of man; that is to say, it is able to move human wills or (as some thinkers prefer to see it, to co-operate with them), so that the individuals concerned are rescued from their sinfulness and enabled to 'grow in grace' and become what God designed them to be. The alteration by grace of the rules which normally govern the running of the natural world is always associated with the divine purpose of perfecting fallen mankind. Thus miracles are seen as designed to capture human attention and win men to faith. They are, as Gregory the Great explains at length in his *Dialogues*, a teaching aid to illuminate human understanding. There can be miraculous consequences of the life of a human being in whom grace is freely at work. Such saints 'perform miracles' throughout mediaeval tradition, and the miracles are taken as signs that they are indeed exceptionally good men and women in whom God has wrought his will. There are healings and the instantaneous multiplication of fishes and other such apparent interferences with the course of nature.

This differs from magic in its wholly edifying purpose and in taking place strictly as God wills, and not at the caprice of a demon. But it is still the case that a miracle appears to break the rules. If it did not do so, it would scarcely capture attention at all. Augustine took the view that we must see such exceptional events not as lying outside the natural rules, but as falling under a higher rule which is itself, ultimately, a rule of nature. Grace can thus be seen not as overriding nature, but as perfecting it: 'gratia non tollit naturam, sed perficit'. That seemed right to Anselm too, and it allows the philosophical contrivance of presenting miracle as in some sense 'natural', so that God does not have to break his own laws to work it.

But even if miracle and the intervention of grace are left out of account, the study of the created world in its mechanical functioning presented Christian thinkers with a number of problems inherited from the philosophers. Much ancient philosophy includes in the attempt to give an account of natural phenomena both questions about the first principles and causes and questions about purpose and ultimate end. On this definition, all sorts of aspects of the dealings of God or the gods with the world are relevant to physics.

But Platonists disagreed with Stoics about the reality-status of things which cannot be perceived by the senses; the Stoics generally taking the view that reality always has some sort of material embodiment. Yet there was broad agreement in dividing the perceptible from the 'intelligible' orders. That passed into the Christian tradition (and was also accepted by Philo).

A difficulty remained about where the line was to be drawn between the science of the perceptible world, whose mechanisms could be studied by means of the senses, and that concerned with the realm of *ingelligibilia*, things which could be known only by the intellect. Platonists tended to distinguish 'God' from 'all created things'. But the higher science might be deemed to include not only God himself but his dealings with the world he had made (that is, such questions as providence, fate, free will). Or it could be thought to cover God himself, and angels, and human souls (except the corrupt). Christian tradition came on the whole to include the area 'above' physics, God and his spiritual creatures, the angels and the souls of men, making the remainder the province of natural science, or *physica*. But there was always overlap, indeed constant interchange, between the two areas of study.

Boethius was important for the Middle Ages as an authority for the definition of physics. Natural science (*physica*) is distinguished from *mathematica* and *theologia*, with the explanation that the province of physics is the forms of bodies taken together with the matter of which they are made, and the motion of such bodies (*De Trinitate*, II). By 'motion' (*motus*) he means the nature which makes them behave as they do. Earth tends downwards; fire tends upwards (*ibid.*), for example.

Physics came into play for theologians in the mediaeval West in the discussion of the created world as it is sustained in being by the Creator. Principles of order and harmony and of hierarchy are crucial here. Eriugena develops them in ways which include many other elements from the philosophical systems on which he draws, but in which we can see the natural 'world in motion' in relation to its Creator.[30] Bede gives us a more pedestrian treatment. God governs the world, which he has made from nothing. The world is the *universitas omnis*, made up of heaven and earth, which is the four elements held in a sphere (*globata*). He describes the structure of the cosmos, planetary motion, the signs of the zodiac, comets, winds, weather, tides, and such other topics as Pliny and Seneca assisted with (*De Natura Rerum*, PL 90.187ff.). The number and arrangement of the heavens gave Carolingians matter for further discussion, and we find arguments about the location of hell, too, in which there is a particular debt to Macrobius.[31]

But we have to wait for the twelfth century before a substantial body of fresh philosophical difficulties became urgent. Peter Lombard deals with the natural world and the structure of the cosmos in his *Sentences* (II, *Dist.* 14). In his *Cosmographia* (i.4), Bernardus Silvestris describes the running of the universe in terms which owe a good deal both to Stoicism and to Neoplatonism. Heat and light, he says, are the moving force of all processes of generation. The light which is God's wisdom radiates from him upon the world, and the laws the Creator has given to nature govern the behaviour of fire and motion. Here, fire is both an element and a force, as for the Stoics. Bernardus follows the *Asclepius* in taking οὐσία to be a synonym for ὕλη, with the result that there is some uncertainty as to whether creation can be said to be the working together of the One and matter, or the One and being. But the elision of the two makes it possible to view divine creativity, and matter, and order, in perpetual interaction, so that the act of creation is repeated again and again throughout the universe and through time. The passage of time itself is regulated by order, and in its turn time regulates the processes of the cosmos. God is the animating presence in Bernardus' *Cosmos*, making the world sentient.

With the advent of Ptolemy's *Almagest*, Aristotle's *De Caelo* and Averroes' commentary on the *De Caelo*, matters became more complicated. Ptolemy describes epicycles and eccentric orbits. Aristotle has homocentric spheres, because it seems to him that self-evident first principles require them in the structure of the universe. Aquinas makes the telling comment that even if Ptolemy's account fits the experimentally verifiable facts better, that does not mean that he is right. Aristotle's first principles are more compelling.[32]

The *Timaeus* suggests an analogy between the structure and working of the cosmos and the nature and behaviour of man. The notion of a macrocosm with which a microcosm has parallels is also to be found in the *Asclepius* (4–8, ed. P. Thomas (Leipzig, 1908), pp. 39–43). Although it occurs in Eriugena, and one or two of the Carolingians after him, the image was not much taken up in the early Middle Ages. It became popular in the twelfth century, when its links with ideas of harmony in the universe, its implications for the existence of a hierarchy in all things, and above all, its suggestion that man is the centre and purpose of the universe were ingeniously exploited. There was some input from Arabic scholarship here. Al-Kindi's *De Radiis* speaks of man as a *minor mundus*, a 'lesser world', in its Latin version, and Bonaventure picks up the phrase in his *Itinerarium Mentis ad Deum*.[33] The study of the natural world could readily be seen on this basis as a necessity for the study of man, and man the centre of the universe and its reason for existing.

The microcosm which man discovers in himself by observation and comparison is seen in the mediaeval period as having an educational purpose. He is to learn from it what the universe is like, and that is to lead him on to a better understanding of the universe's Creator. Bonaventure says that a man has five senses which are like five gates. Through these there enters into his soul a knowledge of things in the sensible world.[34] By reflection on what he learns he sees underlying laws. All things are beautiful and delightful in their own way. Beauty and delightfulness are impossible without proportion. Proportion is fundamentally a matter of number. So everything must be 'full of number' (*numerosa*). Number is therefore an *exemplar* of the Creator.[35] In similar ways divine power, wisdom, goodness, greatness, beauty, fullness and order can be perceived.[36] There was of course nothing new in this line of thinking, but in the wake of twelfth-century exploration of the microcosm theme, thirteenth-century authors came to it afresh. Robert Kilwardby, for example, discusses the 'image' and 'vestige' of the Trinity to be found in creation in a different way from Augustine in his *De Trinitate*. He asks first about the *cognoscibilitas* of such vestiges. Can a creature know them all? What is it in a creature which could arrive at a knowledge of the divine, and how might it do so? He points to analogy as the basis on which that may be possible, for analogy is the basis of the notion of microcosm and macrocosm.

6

MAN

THE SOUL

Genesis 2.7 describes how God breathed life into Adam. That accorded with the consensus of the ancient philosophers that the soul is the animating principle of living beings. That is to say, it is the presence of the soul which makes it possible for the matter of which the body is composed to act as a living thing. Augustine thought the soul was something more. In man the soul is more than mere animator (even vegetables have life). It is more than the power of sensation (which animals also have) (*Conf.* X.7, and see also Boethius on Porphyry on the same point). It is a man's very self, the 'I', says Augustine, 'joined to my body', and by which I fill its frame with life' (*Conf.* X.7).

He fuses two philosophical systems here. Aristotle says that the soul is the form of a natural body which has the potential for life (*De Anima* II.412^{a-3a}). His chief concern was with what we might call the machinery. The Platonists were more interested in trying to understand the relationship between the rational and upwardly aspiring soul and the downward-tugging body to which it gives life, but from which it desires to escape, so that a man is perpetually tugged between the beast and the god in him. The true self of man ought to be above the animal and vegetable.[1] For Augustine as a Christian there is a complex baggage of further connotations, but both these approaches are integral to his.

His principal problem at first was, however, philosophical. He found it hard to understand how the soul could itself be anything other than a body. He describes in the *Confessions* how difficult he found it to grasp the very concept of the incorporeal (III.vii.12; IV.xv.24). Even in the *De Genesi ad Litteram* he still leans to the view that it is a 'sort of substance' (VII.vi.10–11). He had the support of Tertullian and Hilary among the earlier Western Fathers in thinking of the soul in this way, although Augustine himself was convinced it was not the right way to conceive of it. Faustus of Riez pursued the same line in the next generation and Claudianus Mamertus tried to answer him in his *De Statu Animae* (c.467–72) with the argument that the soul cannot be corporeal because it is invisible and has no quantity; moreover, it is in our souls that we are made in the image of God and God has no body, so the soul cannot be a bodily thing. The issue was pursued by Cassiodorus in his *De Anima*, and by Gregory the Great in Book IV of his *Dialogues*, where it is pointed out (as it had been by the Stoics) that one does not see the soul leave the body as one would if it were itself a body. Hincmar of Rheims took up the question again among the Carolingians. It did not disappear even in the thirteenth century, although the questions become increasingly sophisticated. Aquinas discusses in one of his *Quodlibets* whether the soul does not have some sort of 'corporeity'.[2] Questions arise, such as whether the soul will be able to feel the fire of hell in a 'bodily' way, that is, as one would feel it if one were burnt in the body. (Aquinas says no. But it will be able to 'feel' the fire as an instrument of divine avenging justice.)[3]

The underlying philosophical problem here is the classic one of the possibility of a relationship between spiritual and material which had made many philosophers in the ancient world disinclined to believe that the immutable Supreme Being could have anything to do with a creation which had all the most disparaged attributes of the material and bodily: the capacity to change and decay, the tendency to fall away from the Highest at every point. In miniature we have a similar problem about the soul's continuing in a working relationship with the body unless it is itself somehow 'bodily'.

Certainly any relationship between body and soul ought to make the soul the body's master. Plato's view that the spiritual is intrinsically higher and finer than the corporeal was pervasive in the Christian tradition too. Hermetic thinking stressed that a man who cultivates his spiritual nature will grow more Godlike, while one who behaves like a beast will degenerate into a lowlier, 'bodily' condition. The soul ought to keep the body in subjection (and here St Paul would come naturally to the mind of the Christian theologian). It ought, as William of Auvergne puts it in his *De Anima*, to behave like the king of a kingdom, keeping the lower powers of its bodily nature under control, making reason the king's councillor, sending other powers to do his bidding at his will and making the senses inspectors which travel about and report what they see faithfully to their king.[4]

A number of more or less mechanical questions were seen to arise. In his *De Quantitate Animi* Augustine had asked various questions which were also of interest to Plotinus: whether the soul fills the body, as it were to the fingertips. If it does, what happens when a limb is amputated? Is part of the soul lost too? Or does the remainder of the body still contain the whole soul? Is the soul related to the body as form to matter? asks Gilbert of Poitiers, even before the arrival of the *libri naturales* of Aristotle in the Western schoolroom. Further detailed questions of physics presented themselves from the thirteenth century. Aquinas, for example, wrestles with the question of what moves the heart. It is not easy to see how it can be the soul, for in its nutritive function the soul only generates, digests, grows, shrinks, and in its sensitive and intellective functions, proper to animals and man respectively, it moves by desire, while the *motus cordis* is involuntary. Such interesting enquiries were multiplied in the thirteenth-century schools as Aristotle's *De Anima* became the first work of Aristotelian science to which students were normally introduced.

Even if the question of the intrinsic incompatibility of soul and body can be resolved, we are immediately brought up against the opposite difficulty: if it seems that man is both body and soul, can the soul be separated from the body at death, even temporarily, without destroying human fullness of being? This was an urgent question for Christian thinkers, because of the doctrine of the resurrection of the body which appears in Paul and in early creeds. It was more or less universally accepted by mediaeval theologians that when someone dies he is separated from his body, but at the Last Judgement he will be reunited with it, and only then can he enter fully into the bliss of heaven. This belief prompted a multitude of questions about what happens to the soul in the period after death and before the resurrection of the body,[5] whether during this time it is possible for the individual to be truly himself, and how it may be possible for the separated soul to perceive what is happening around it, while it lacks the bodily sense to inform it. There were also questions about the form the resurrected body would take. Origen did not think it would be spherical, as some said, and in fact that view was condemned at the Council of Constantinople in 533.[6] But mediaeval debate explored increasingly complex questions in this area. Giles of Rome, for example, draws on Aristotle to ask whether the agent intellect can remain in the soul when it is separated from the body.

The origin of the soul

The Pythagoreans believed the human soul to be some sort of divine spark, a fragment of heavenly origin embedded in matter. Augustine specifically condemns this view in the *De Genesi ad Litteram* (VII.2, 3 and 5, 7). From the Christian point of view it had the disadvantage of implying that God is not ultimately separate from, and other than, his creatures, and of being cognate with the theory of the world-soul in some of its forms. Gnostic and later Manichee tradition took the idea up, with the modification that the divine spark is seen as a fallen spiritual being, trapped in the body as a punishment for sin, and under the imperative to free itself and return to its proper purely spiritual state. Here again, Christian thinkers met something they could not accept, because it was incompatible with the belief that a human being is created to be both a bodily and a spiritual creature. The captive divine spark owes something in its conception to the Platonic theory of the trans-migration of souls. This, too, was unacceptable to Christians because it went against the understanding that each human being lives one life on earth which determines his eternal destiny. Despite the objections to each of these hypotheses which gradually became clear, some patristic authors before Augustine did toy with them. But on the whole, after the fourth century, they disappear from Christian writers, in favour of a more settled Christian understanding that the soul of each human being is uniquely his own; that it lives one life on earth in the body, and will be reunited with that body at the end of the world; that it is a spiritual substance and immortal.

Nevertheless, the question of the origin of the soul was not fully resolved by Christian theologians during the Middle Ages. It was never settled, by Augustine or his successors, whether each soul was freshly created when a child was conceived, or whether the soul was somehow generated with the body. Bede reflects on the problem in his *De Natura Rerum* (*PL* 90.190–1), and Carolingian commentators were aware that neither Augustine nor Jerome had given a ruling.[7] The lack of Augusti-nian guidance on this point was important from an early date. Cassiodorus says that it is Augustine's opinion that it is impossible to determine whether the Creator makes new souls for new bodies, or whether souls are generated with bodies in the natural process of the begetting and bearing of children (*De Anima*, VII, *PL* 70.1292). Alcuin thinks it best to leave not only this but many other problems connected with the soul a mystery known only to God (*PL* 101.645). Christian and pagan thinkers alike have failed to settle matters (*ibid.*). Augustine consulted Jerome, says Alcuin, and neither could determine matters so that future generations know what to think (*ibid.*). Rabanus Maurus, the Carolingian encyclopaedist, presses the view that Augustine was right to have said he was unsure (*PL* 110.1112).

The difficulty in deciding between a traducianist and a creationist view is, as Gregory the Great pointed out, that if souls are generated with bodies, it is hard to see why they do not die when the body dies. If, on the other hand, they are freshly created for each child, why are they tainted with original sin (*Epistolae, MHG Epist.* II.147.13 (IX.147), to Secondinus, May 599)?

Perhaps the most substantial attempt to resolve the Augustinian dilemma was that of Anselm of Canterbury. He did not live to write the study he projected, saying wistfully on his death-bed that he wished he could live long enough to solve the problem of the origin of the soul, for he did not know who could do so when he was dead. But he had published a good deal on the subject already. While he was writing the *Cur Deus Homo* he had set aside the problem of the way in which it could be possible for God to become, not man, but sinless man, when the whole human race is tainted with sin. He returned to it in a separate treatise, the *De Conceptu Virginali.* It seemed to him that the question of the origin of the soul must turn on the solution to the problem of the transmission of original sin (S II.140.5). As Anselm sees it, the origin of sin cannot lie in human nature, for Adam and Eve were at first without sin (S II.140.12–14). Original sin is therefore 'original' to each individual; that is, it originates in the individual. Anselm distinguishes here between the *natura* which all men have in common, and the *persona* which individuates. Original sin in the individual, although it comes to taint his human nature, can be present only when there is a human person (S II.140.24–6), that is, when there is an individual man. Anselm wants to separate the bodily conception of an infant from the arrival of the rational soul. We know, he says, from Scripture, that original sin is not present from the moment of conception (S II.148.10–16). So when the Virgin conceived, there was no sin in her child's body. In Jesus, the individuating Person united from the first both divine and human nature and so the rational soul in him could not be the source of original sin. In ordinary humanity it is always the case (arguably with the exception of the Blessed Virgin) that as the foetus develops, a blueprint unfolds which means that as it becomes a person with the arrival of the rational soul, the new human being will be tainted with original sin (S II.149.1–5).

What Anselm achieved here was an explanation which makes it unnecessary to stipulate either that the soul is generated with the body or that it is freshly created. The question was repeatedly raised in later mediaeval centuries. A thirteenth-century set of questions on the soul (possibly by Matthew of Aquasparta, who died in 1302) asks specifically whether the 'intellective soul' is generated or created. He cites Aristotle, Porphyry and Pseudo-Dionysius in favour of generation. The author himself is disposed to think the creationist view is right.

SAVING MAN

The *Asclepius* describes man as poised between God and beast in his nature, because he is both a bodily and a spiritual creature. We have already touched on this hermetic tradition that if man behaves in accordance with his lower nature, he will grow more like a beast. If he cultivates his soul, he will grow more God-like. That puts crudely a widespread notion of late Platonism that the human condition is a perpetual struggle between a debasing materialism and an elevating spirituality, conceived of as primarily intellectual. There are traces of it in Augustine, in his famous phrase: *deificari in otio*, in which he describes the ascent of the soul towards God through a leisure spent in philosophical contemplation. There is a fundamental problem here for Christian thought. The pagan philosopher has no difficulty with the idea that a man might thus become a god, although he will draw the line at talk of a man's attaining to the heights of a divine 'being above being'. The Christian can speak only of man's return to the way he was made: in the image and likeness of God (Genesis 1.26). Man cannot become God.

There is, however, a starting-point here for a tradition of mediaeval mysticism which envisages a goal of union with God such as Bernard of Clairvaux describes, and which was the experience of many later mediaeval mystics. Such union is, as a rule, only momentary. It is seen as a foretaste of heaven, when the lover of God will be united with him for ever in a bliss of contemplation.

From Augustine onwards 'becoming God-like' in this way is seen as an intellectual bliss, a perfection of mutual understanding. A singular exception is Anselm, who thinks there will be room for many familiar physical and emotional pleasures in heaven. More typical is Ailred of Rievaulx, in whose treatise on spiritual friendship is a picture of a shared understanding between Christians in this life in which Christ is always present too. Such conceptions of heaven and its first fruits on earth depend upon Platonism's ideal of reason transfigured, able to see clearly the supreme Reason which is its pattern and to enjoy purely intellectual joys untainted by the urgencies of the demands of the flesh.

Pseudo-Dionysius worked out the implications of this doctrine of a return to God by means of a purified intelligence in some detail, and this thinking was an important source of a number of mediaeval assumptions in this area. He saw the whole hierarchical structure of the universe as a ladder designed to help the soul of man in its spiritual climb. The process of perfecting requires the soul to climb step by step; there can be no direct ascent. Down the steps flows the influence of the divine, which is itself the cause of the order, knowledge and activity of which the hierarchy is composed. Up the steps proceeds the soul, gaining ever greater illumination as it is purified and comes closer to God, and able to begin at all only because God comes down to meet it, and to show it the way.

All sorts of uses were made of this model. It seemed to be in keeping with the image of Jacob's Ladder (Genesis 28.12), which was always popular with mediaeval writers on spirituality, and so it caused no substantial difficulties in Christian use. Pseudo-Dionysius himself employs the image to explain why there are three orders of ordained minister. Deacons are responsible for purifying, priests for illuminating and bishops for perfecting the souls in their charge. Bernard of Clairvaux wrote (drawing here on Benedict too) on the steps of pride and humility the soul descends and ascends on its way to heaven. Alan of Lille makes the image the basis of a criticism of the way the beastly-minded drag down the study of theology to their own level. Their intellectual bestiality makes them scarcely capable of comprehending a piece of theatre, and they pretend to understand the debates of angels and even the colloquies of God.

Alan of Lille also touches on the theme in his *Regulae Theologiae*. *Regulae* V and VI deal with the question of beginning and end in relation to the Godhead. God is, as Monad, the beginning and end of all things, for all things tend to One as to their last end (V). Every creature, having a beginning and end, is capable of dissolution, even the angels. But while all created things are good in their beginning, for God made them, only rational creatures are good in both their beginning and their end, for the rational creatures not only tend towards God, but worship him, love him (VI).

But for the Christian, the notion of a return to God depends on the work of Christ. Here philosophy had been relevant if often embarrassing in the early Christian centuries. The idea that God might become man and enter this world to save sinners was quite foreign, indeed repugnant, to Platonism. But the philosophical traditions had had something to contribute to the debate about the manner in which the Incarnation could be possible. Boethius, especially, made use of them in his *Contra Eutychen*, where he explores all the options he can see, by way of 'mixing' and 'conjunction', and so on, in an attempt to provide a solid philosophical basis for the Chalcedonian view that Christ was one Person in two natures.

Peter Abelard in the twelfth century stresses the usefulness of the philosophers' concepts of the *Logos* as *sapientia, sophia, lumen, mens*. He got himself into trouble by doing so, because he seemed in danger of tumbling into old heresies about the distinction of attributes of the Godhead into those common to God as one and those proper to the Persons individually (see, for example, *CCCM*, XII, p. 293).

Yet, on the negative side, the revival of interest in philosophical vocabulary and frames of reference meant a corresponding revival of old heresies, sometimes in new guides. The author of the diatribe *Against the Four Labyrinths* of France, in the late twelfth century, speaks of 'new heretics' who say that Christ is nothing in so far as he is man ('non esse aliquid in eo quod est homo'), and others who say it is unfitting to suggest that God could be anything which he was not always, and that the Son cannot therefore have become incarnate at some point in history.

On the question of what was effected for man's salvation by the life and death and resurrection of Christ, philosophy had little to contribute directly, although Anselm attempted in his *Cur Deus Homo* to demonstrate by pure reason why God became man.

SACRAMENT

Much of what has been said in this study has perforce been general, and it has been possible to give only a few illustrations. It would be a pity not to include a closer case study, to illustrate something of the texture of the philosophical treatment of theological problems in the Middle Ages. A convenient case in point is the controversy over the Eucharist, out of which the doctrine of transubstantiation evolved in the course of the eleventh and twelfth centuries.

This debate constituted in fact only one area of a much fuller discussion of the saving power of the sacraments in the Church, which was to run on into the Reformation and beyond. It was agreed in the Middle Ages that Christ had instituted baptism and the Lord's Supper as means of grace, that is, as a 'trust' of which the Church was steward, through which the Holy Spirit could work in a regular and orderly way in the lives of God's people. The theology of baptism was relatively uncontroversial. Infant baptism became the norm in the West after the fourth century. Administered in the name of the Trinity and with water, and with a profession of faith made on behalf of the candidate, which the candidate made for himself when he was old enough, baptism was understood to remove once and for all the guilt of original sin, and all penalties of actual sins committed before baptism. The unbaptised could not, it was generally held, be saved. The Eucharist was increasingly seen as a means of applying the saving work of Christ in his death to the needs of sinners who accumulated the penalties for fresh sins throughout their lives, and needed to find forgiveness for them.

The precise relationship between the body of Christ as he died on the Cross, his risen body in heaven, and the bread consecrated as his body in the Mass therefore became important. From the eleventh century until the fifteenth it was usual to speak of the 'true body and blood' of Christ in the Eucharist, rather than of the 'real presence'. This emphasis created a preoccupation with the physics and metaphysics of the manner in which the bread and wine became body and blood, and gave rise to debates of ever-increasing technical complexity as scholars got to grips with Aristotelian physics in the high Middle Ages. The word 'true' threw its own shadow epistemologically, and in terms of the vastly more sophisticated signification theory of centuries beyond the eleventh, over the debates about analogy, and the figurative use of words and things.

Between 1050 and 1079 the grammarian Berengar and Lanfranc of Bec, who later became Archbishop of Canterbury, with a number of other scholars in succeeding decades, were engaged in a dispute over the exact nature of the change. Berengar was brought on two occasions to agree that the bread and wine become 'true body and blood'. In the first recantation that is taken to mean that they are capable of being 'in truth' handled by the priest and broken, and attacked by the teeth of the faithful.[8] That seems to imply a rough equation of bodily reality with tangibility. In the second we find the statement that the change takes place *substantialiter*, and the reference to touching has gone.[9] That may be partly because of pressure on the discussion already being generated by a question which was to become by far the most common on this subject in the circle of the Cathedral school at Laon at the end of the century: whether at the Last Supper itself Christ gave his mortal and passible body, as it was then, or his incorruptible body, as it is now; if the former, the act of breaking and tearing would be a fearsome matter. In any case, it shifts into sharp focus the issue of 'substance'.

Two existing bodies of discussion would have come naturally to mind in this connection. The first is the Augustinian legacy of vocabulary and concepts developed in debating the question of one substance and three Persons in the Trinity. We find Berengar himself discussing this, and it was raised by William of Champeaux too.[10] Augustine could use 'substance' (*substantia*) interchangeably with 'essence' (*essentia*) and 'nature' (*natura*) in this area, and we find all three terms among the anti-Berengarian authors.[11]

The second authority to which it would be natural to turn was Aristotle–Boethius. In thinking about the application of the *Categoria* to the divine there was Augustinian as well as Boethian precedent for the clear understanding that God presents a special case. We find William of Champeaux reflecting on the application of 'quality' and of 'doing' and 'suffering', for example;[12] quantity arises everywhere because of the puzzle as to how one body can make so many hosts; time and place present difficulties because of Christ's presence not only everywhere and at all times in the Eucharists upon earth, but also simultaneously in heaven; relation is discussed by Alger of Liège.[13] William of St Thierry expresses the special character of talk of the *categories* in relation to the Eucharist in various ways. He points out that while in ordinary cases the substance 'makes' the accidents (*efficit*), that is not so in the Mass. The body of Christ in its actual substance (*quantum in sua substantia*) does not make the whiteness of the bread white or its roundness round.[14] In answer to the question whether anything changes in the quality of Christ's substance, for he becomes, it seems, tractable and able to be tasted (*tractabile et gustabile*), he reminds us that God's substance in itself is good without quality; it is great without quantity; it is omnipresent without place.[15] That is to say, when the substance of the bread changes into the substance of the body of Christ, all the 'attributes' of Christ (to use the term improperly) are present in the substance of his body, and although the bread is left as accidents without substance, Christ is not incomplete when his substance is present, as it were, without accidents. (It was suggested elsewhere that even the bread and wine do not 'perish', for to 'change into another substance' is not to perish.)[16]

Part of the discussion turned on the 'substances' (plural) of the bread and wine. Lanfranc and others after him distinguish between the species (that is, the bread and wine) and 'certain other qualities' (such as flavour, roundness) in his comments on these.[17] The burning issue here – a pastoral one in origin – was whether if one of the faithful received only wine (as was common for young children), or only bread (for 'peasants', *rustici*), he or she had received less than someone who received both elements; or conversely, whether to receive both was to receive something extra.[18] William of Champeaux tries to explain that in each species, bread and wine, there is the whole Christ (who since the Resurrection is

Nyack College Library

invisible, impassible and indivisible), in such a way that the blood is not without flesh (*sine carne*) and the flesh not bloodless (*sine sanguine*), and neither is without the human soul of Christ; and that total human nature of Christ is never 'without the Word personally joined with it' ('sine verbo Deo sibi personaliter counito').[19] 'Substance' would seem to be used in a straightforward, physical way, in speaking of the bread and wine as 'substances', but something very different is to be understood of the divine substance which is not only the body of Christ, but his blood, his soul, and whole human nature the Word of God. Many mid-twelfth-century questions were asked in this area: about whether the transubstantiation (*transubstantiatio*) of the bread took place before that of the wine, and if so, whether the Eucharist could be complete without the wine; when exactly in the process of consecration the change was made, of bread-substance and of wine-substance.[20]

But the heart of the matter, of course, was the nature of the change itself. Some authors avoid the technical question with a vague term such as 'turned' (*vertitur*).[21] Robert of Melun tries to be more exact. It is not, he says, a case of the bread being taken away and the body of Christ being put in its place.[22] To say that would be heresy. One substance passes (*transit*) into the other, but Robert is not prepared to say whether that happens all at once or bit by bit (*tota in totam* or *partes in partes*).[23] Master Simon in his *De Sacramentis* speaks of *commutatio* rather than *transubstantiatio*, 'an ineffable commutation of substance into substance'. We believe, he explains, that 'under' those same accidents 'under' which the bread was before, now 'the body of Christ is'. That is not, he insists, to say that the body of Christ is made 'of the bread' (*ex pane*).[24] Simon of Tournei, who was one of the first, perhaps the first, to use the word *transubstantiatio*, explains that the bread does not change into the blood or the wine into the body, and neither changes 'into Christ' (*in Christum*), and yet the whole Christ (*totus Christus*) is received in each.[25] The most elaborate attempt to explain the change is in Alan of Lille's *Regulae Theologicae*. Rule 107 seeks to distinguish between *alteratio*, *alteritas* and *transubstantiatio*. 'Alteration' of substance takes place according to 'accidental' properties, as when black becomes white. So one might say 'black becomes white', but not 'white is made from black'. *Alteritas* involves a change of substance in substantial respects (*secundum substantialia*). That is what happened at the wedding at Cana in Galilee, where water became wine. Here we say 'Wine is made from water.' In transubstantiation, neither the matter (*materia*) nor the 'substantial form' (*substantialis forma*) remains, but only the *accidentalia*. Thus we can say 'the bread becomes the body of

Christ' (*fiet*); it is *mutabiliter*, by change, converted (*convertetur*) into the body of Christ. We may not say that the bread 'will be the body of Christ', or that it 'begins to be' (*incipiet esse*), or that it is made from the bread (*de pane fiet*). We can say that it becomes (*fiet*) his body.[26]

Guitmund of Aversa tells us that even at the date when he was writing not all those who might be called 'Berengarians' think the same. Some say that the body of Christ is present in a hidden way in the bread, 'so to speak, impanated' ('ut ita dixerim, impanari').[27] They say that this is the more subtle meaning (*subtilior sensus*) of Berengar's teaching. Contained in it in a hidden way (*latenter contineri*), the true body does not replace the substance of the bread. This view was upheld in different words by Rupert of Deutz between 1112 and 1117. Just as the human nature was not destroyed when Christ became incarnate, but joined with the divine in unity of person, so the substance of bread and wine is not changed or destroyed, but conjoined in unity with the body which hung on the Cross and the blood which flowed from Christ's side,[28] he argues. The neologism *impanari* is clearly intended to echo *incarnari*. Rupert's contemporaries, like Guitmund, were uneasy about using it. Alger of Liège, who was quick to attack Rupert, weakens it by adding 'as if' ('quasi impanatum');[29] William of St Thierry, who questioned Rupert's position soon afterwards, qualifies it too. 'If it could be said, it would be said that the Word was not only incarnate, but impanated.'[30]

The key objection to this position according to William of St Thierry is that the idea that the bread remains has always been abhorrent to Christians and was recently condemned in Berengar's teaching.[31] In fact, the objection proved to lie elsewhere, both for Alger and for William. Alger baulks at the notion that, just as the Word became flesh, so bread becomes that same flesh.[32] There is a confusion of comparisons (*confusio similitudinum*) here, he says, for the 'becoming' is quite different in each case (*longe diverso modo*); he points out some of the differences. The bread is not born. In the womb Christ took the species or form of man with the substance, but on the altar he takes the species or form of the bread without the substance. When Scripture calls the Lord's body 'bread' ('I am the bread of life'), it speaks figuratively, not 'substantially' (*non substantialiter*).[33] How can Christ be said to be 'impanated' when he is not turned into bread and in no way becomes bread?[34] The elements do not become one person with Christ.[35] He puts the confusion down not merely to a mistake about the analogy to be drawn between two 'becomings', but to the reading of a grammatical similarity, that is, a similarity in the form of words, for a similarity of understanding or sense.[36] A better comparison would be between a man and a picture of a man (an example from Aristotle). We say of both 'that is the man'. He concedes that the figure of the bread (*figura panis*) has a closer generic likeness to the body of Christ (*familior*) than a picture has to a man.[37] There seems here to be an underlying sense of the indignity and inappropriateness of Christ's becoming personally impanated in bread (*personaliter in pane impanatum*), as he was personally incarnate in human flesh.[38] Alger does not examine the anomalies which would arise from the whole incarnate Christ becoming impanated, but treats the question at issue as though it were a matter of the Son's becoming 'bread' as he became 'man'; he does not take in here the principles already referred to which are outlined by William of Champeaux.[39]

William of St Thierry takes us beyond the simple 'contained in a hidden way' (*latenter contineri*) of Guitmund, and Alger's elaborate refutation of Rupert's parallel between Incarnation and 'imputation', to the idea of 'inherence in'. He sees it as orthodox and acceptable to say that the accidents which inhere in (*pani inhaerens*) the original bread migrate to the substance of the body of Christ and inhere there.[40] This assumes that the substance of the bread is thus left out of account. But 'inherence' is in itself a concept which takes us beyond a crude 'hiding inside'.

It is reasonably asked what the accidents of the bread can be said to be 'in' when the substance of the bread is gone. They are not in the bread. Nor are they in the body of Christ. The *Ysagoge in Theologiam* of the school of Abelard suggests that God can cause them to continue in being without any substance.[41] Master Simon replies to those who think they are 'in' the air that that would mean that they would appear to shift about with the movement of the air. It is wiser (*sanius*), he thinks, to believe that they are 'in' no substance at all, but subsist on their own (*per se subsistunt*) to aid the faithful.[42]

Thus from a doctrine of change in the substance of the elements was seen to arise a variety of anomalies and difficulties. These were raised not necessarily by 'Berengarians', but, as is clear from the texts of the 'school' of Anselm of Laon, in the course of honest enquiry by students and scholars. The intention was not to overthrow the teaching of the Church but to understand how it could be right and at the same time incomprehensible. The result of such questioning – coupled with that of those who were indeed of Berengar's opinion or something like it – was to clarify many details and make the official doctrine altogether more hard-edged over the decades at the end of the eleventh and the beginning of the twelfth century when it was the subject of active controversy.

A major question was which 'body of Christ' the bread and wine became. As William of St Thierry was to point out, 'the body of Christ' had at least three senses. It could refer to the body which hung on the Cross, the historical body of Christ, which in his view is also the body which is sacrificed on the altar. It could refer to the body which, when the believer eats it, brings eternal life. It could mean the Church.[43] But these three, he explains, are really one, the same body considered with respect to its essence (*secundum essentiam*), with respect to its unity (*secundum unitatem*) and with respect to its effect (*secundum effectum*).[44] The continuing concern of Berengar's opponents almost from the beginning was to insist that the body of Christ into which the bread was transformed in the Eucharist was the self-same, historical body, in which he had lived and died. That meant it was no mere figurative change, or figurative body. Gilbert Crispin's way of putting it is to say that it is one and the same numerically (*unum et idem numerum*), a Boethian phrase.[45] Gilbert and Durandus both refer to the idea that at the Last Supper Christ carried himself in his hands, and at the same time was carried in his own hands.[46] This is, says Gilbert, no more remarkable than the soul's being in different parts of the body at the same time. But even if, as Anselm of Laon says, 'No sane person is in doubt about the truth of the substance', there remains a difficulty about the doctrine that the Eucharistic 'body' is Christ's historical body, which he is less confident is to be easily resolved. Did Christ give himself to his disciples at the Last Supper as he then was, mortal and corruptible (*corruptibile*) or as he was to be, incorruptible (*incorruptibile*)? Here there is some dispute even among the orthodox.[47] He judges it better to think that Jesus gave himself to his disciples as he then was.[48] Did the disciples, then, receive his mortal body? Yes, thinks Anselm of Laon, but we receive it as it is now, the same historical body, but immortal.[49]

Whether mortal and corruptible, or immortal and incorruptible, the historical body of Christ would seem to be, by definition, of a sort of substance which is quantitative and subject to location. So at least it seemed to those engaged in the debate and anxious to reconcile this assumption with a doctrine of a literal and physical substantial change. At the Last Supper the whole Christ bore himself in his hands, and it was the whole Christ he carried.[50] When some object that an unimaginably huge 'body' would be needed to make all the hosts for so many Eucharists, Guitmund replies that those hosts are not 'parts' of the body of Christ, but themselves that whole body.[51] There are no little portions (*portiunculae*) of the sort described mockingly by Berengar.[52] Alger too emphasises that when the body of Christ is broken and received by the faithful in the Eucharist, it remains whole and undiminished.[53] Durandus makes the same point.[54] To this paradox our authors added another. When Christ sat at the table at the Last Supper, he was wholly there, says Gilbert, but he was also wholly in the mouths of those who were eating the bread which was his body.[55] There is no difference, he maintains, between that bilocation and Christ's now being in heaven and at the same time in the host.[56] Alger stresses that the body of Christ is locally in heaven and also locally on earth.[57] Lanfranc, making the same point, says that this is a mystery to which we must bow, much as it affronts reason.[58] Both the laws which normally govern physical quantity and those which govern physical location are broken. Both are involved in the miracle that Christ is attacked by the teeth of the faithful and yet remains whole and undamaged. All this 'goes beyond the nature of substance in a body',[59] comments Gilbert. Every corporeal substance (*corporea substantia*) is *circumscripta*, finite, and it cannot be completely in several places. The method by which the defenders of the Church's position tackle these fearsome anomalies is, then, to acknowledge them freely, but to hold them up to the faithful as wonders, whose miraculous character should increase their faith, not cause them to doubt that there is a real substantial change.

The miraculous character of the change is freely discussed. It is compared with the power by which God created the world out of nothing. To change one thing into another seems less of a wonder than that. It is also (though less generally) compared with the miracle of the Incarnation.[60] Moreover, the food we eat turns into our bodies every day.[61] But if the argument rests in the end on the contention that the very anomalies are themselves wonderful, and meant to awaken us to faith, some put forward the difficulties about 'indignity', which seem to point the other way. 'Perish the thought that it should be right for Christ to be torn by teeth!' exclaims Guitmund's interlocutor Roger, in his debate with Guitmund.[62] If our opponents the Berengarians want to say that that is undignified, answers Guitmund, what will they say of the humiliation which Christ willingly underwent when, for our salvation, he was beaten, wore a crown of thorns, and was torn by the Cross, the nails, the spear?[63] Certainly it seems unacceptable to think of the 'substances of the divine oblation' as capable of being digested, indeed of causing indigestion and drunkenness if taken to excess, just like any other bread and wine, as the Berengarians would have it.[64] (One compromise suggestion came from William of Champeaux. He suggests that it is the species of the bread and wine which remain which are chewed, but the substance itself, the body of Christ, remains whole.)[65] In such ways the objection that it would be undignified to become Christ's body is turned on its head.

One of the strongest arguments in favour of the view that there is, metaphysically speaking, a real change, is that that makes it easier to understand the effect of the Eucharist. Guitmund describes it as a 'saving effect' (*nostrae salutis effectivum*).[66] Durandus is more explicit. Those who ate manna in the desert died. Our miraculous food is the living Bread who came down from heaven, the body of Christ, and it gives us the substance of eternal life (*vitae aeternae substantiam subministrat*).[67] We remain naturally (*naturaliter*) in Christ through participation (*per commercium*) in his holy flesh (*sanctae suae carnis*), and he in us through his assumption of our weakness. He has incorporated us powerfully into himself (*nos sibi potenter corporavit*) and makes us naturally (*naturaliter*) one with him by communication in his body and blood with him.[68] This same theme of union with Christ is emphasised by Alger[69] and Anselm of Laon.[70]

But against any doctrine of 'automatic' incorporation resulting from the physical reality of the body of Christ which the believer receives were raised questions about the need for worthiness in the minister,[71] and for worthiness in the person receiving.[72]

The power of the words of consecration (*vis verborum*) was of central importance for our authors. Lanfranc points out that if there is such *vis in sermone* in Jesus that things could come into being which did not exist before, how much more easily could he cause what was already there to change into something else.[73] Durandus puts it in terms of 'before' and 'after'. Before the words of Christ, the cup is full of wine and water. When those words have done their work, there is the blood which redeems his people.[74] Alger of Liège speaks in similar terms of the power of the words of consecration.[75] 'Through' (*per*) the words, says Anselm of Laon, the bread is changed (*commutari*) into the body of Christ.[76]

This sort of thinking about the effect of words is in line with contemporary understanding of what at a later date it would be appropriate to call the theory of signification. Guitmund describes Berengar's position as being that the bread and wine are not truly and substantially (*vere substantialiterque*) the body and the blood but 'merely so-called by name' (*sola voce sic appellari*), the shadow and figure being themselves significative (*significativa*) of the body and blood, that is, acting as signs in their own right.[77] There is some play with the vocabulary of 'naming' in Durandus. 'It is said to be flesh (*dicitur*) and it is called bread (*vocatur*); bread, because it is food, or because of its outward appearance; flesh, because it is life, and because of the truth lying hidden in it (*latentum*) by an inward dispensation (*intrinsecus dispensatione*).[78] Again: before the blessing of the heavenly words, it is named as a species (*alia species nominatur*); after the consecration the body of Christ is signified' (*significatur*). Before the consecration the wine is said to be one thing (*aliud dicitur*); after the consecration it is called blood (*sanguis nuncupatur*).[79] There are no exact technical distinctions here. The variation of terms seems to be designed to avoid repetition; this is stylistic. But underlying all the words for naming is the key recognition that 'After Christ had blessed the bread he did not call it bread but body.'[80]

This tempted comparison with other occasions when Christ had called himself the 'vine' or the 'way'. If 'I am the vine', *ego sum vitis*, is said in the same way as 'this is my body', should they be taken in the same sense (*eodem sensu*)? asks Gilbert. If so, either the bread is only figuratively or significatively the body of Christ; or he is substantially (*substantialiter*) the vine, and that is not what catholic faith believes.[81] It cannot necessarily be the case that things said in the same form of words[82] have to be taken in the same sense. Sheer shortage of words may cause us to use equivocation. We say that the Jews crucified the Lord, but in fact it was the gentiles.[83] If we examine the different ways in which Christ 'is' man, or a lion, we see that he is a man in nature, a lion in action. So 'is' may tell us to take the sense *significative* or *substantive*, depending on the context. Jesus himself explained in the case of his figurative 'is' exactly what he meant, after he had made the statement 'I am the vine', etc. It was a very different matter in the case of the bread and the wine. There, there is no explanation of a figure, and we must take it that he meant what he said literally.[84]

Further questions arising from contemporary grammatical and logical studies also arose. Should the bread be said to be called the body of Christ 'properly' or in a simile (*similitudinarie*)?[85] Alger thinks that in this unique case, it is something between the two. It is acceptable to say that it is a proper usage, but it is said, nevertheless, somewhat improperly (*aliquantulum improprie*), because the form and qualities of the bread remain.[86] The substance is transferred (*translata est*), and some transference (*translatio*) of usage must go with it.[87] The use of *transferre* for the change in substance is of some interest, because *translatio* was a standard term for a transference of signification from literal to metaphorical or vice versa. We find a borrowing the opposite way in talk of the category of relation (*ad aliquid*) in the context of usage. 'These words are relative', says Lanfranc.[88] He is trying to explain away the difficulty to which Berengar points, that in Scripture there is reference to *species*, *similitudo*, *figura*, *signum*, *mysterium*, *sacramentum* in speaking of the bread.[89]

Over all broods the consciousness of the enormous and complex problems raised by Scriptural usage.[90] Lanfranc comments that when 'bread' is referred to, that is the custom of the Scripture's way of speaking.[91] In the Bible it is common for things to be called by the names of those things from which they come or are made, or by the names of what they are merely thought to be.[92] 'What is the definition of a figurative saying?' (*definitio figuratae locutionis*) asks Rupert. He explains that when the word sounds as though it means one thing and something else is to be understood, that is a figurative saying. In the case of 'This is my body' the *figuratio* disappears, and the *sensus verbi consonus*, the sense of the word as it sounds, remains, that is, that the bread is converted into the true substance of his body by divine power.[93] It is, in other words, the reverse of a figurative saying, for in this supremely special usage of Scripture, the words mean exactly what they say. Gilbert Crispin does not think it so straightforward. He sees a paradox. 'We do not utterly exclude the figure from this sacrament, nor admit it to be only a figure. It is true because it is the body of Christ. It is a figure, because what is incorruptible is sacrificed.' If the *hoc* was not substantive, he says, the words 'given for you' would only be figurative.[94]

All Berengar's accusers struggle with paradox. If we are to say he is wrong in speaking of the bread and wine as 'only a sacrament', we do not want to deny that they are a sacrament. Guitmund asks 'if it is a figure, how is it true?'[95] Durandus tries to explain how Christ in the Eucharist is *verus homo*, even though he is said to be in the 'likeness of man' in Scripture. *Figura* does not rule out *substantia*, he insists. It is not *substantiae abnegativa*.[96] Alger says that a body which is spiritual and invisible may also be substantial and 'true'.[97] It is the body Christ had from the virgin which we receive, and yet it is not (*et tamen non ipsum*), says Lanfranc.[98]

It was evidently asked why God should choose so extraordinary a device as transubstantiation. Lanfranc says that it is an act of kindness on the Lord's part, for if the faithful saw the flesh and blood, they would be filled with horror. It is also a test of faith, for those who believe without seeing deserve the greater reward.[99] The same point is made by Alger. If the bread vanished altogether it would be so apparent that a miracle had taken place that there would be no work left for faith to do.[100] There is the further possibility that it is a teaching aid. Berengar had pointed out that if the host were kept long enough it would grow mouldy. Guitmund answers that if that were to happen it would either be an indication that there had been some *negligentia* on the part of the ministers, or a sign to test the faith of the people, or perhaps to prove that it had been insufficient.[101] The further reason usually added by the mid-twelfth century was so that unbelievers might not laugh to see Christians drinking blood.[102] But we may look at the question in a rather different way in the light of the influence of the assumptions and methods of ancient philosophy which we have seen running so strongly through the controversy. To some degree that heritage presented the difficulty and shaped the reply it was possible to make to it.

ETHICS AND POLITICS

The Scriptures provided ample material for discussion about the good Christian life, and moral philosophy was for many centuries largely subsumed in mediaeval Christian teaching on the virtues and vices. Prudentius provided a literary model in his *Psychomachia* (written in Augustine's lifetime), in the form of an allegorical battle between personified virtues and vices. (Alan of Lille made use of that idea in his late twelfth-century poem *Anticlaudianus*, and there are a number of other mediaeval imitations.) But as we have seen, something akin to a notion of philosophy as a guide of life, and thus of Christianity itself as a 'philosophy', persisted in some authors. Peter Abelard, for example, says that we are truly 'philosophers' if we love Christ (*CCCM*, XII.149).

Philosophia Moralis was characteristically divided into those aspects of right living which concern one's relations with fellow-citizens and subjects, and which may be described as 'political'; those which have to do with family life and are called 'economic'; and those which concern the inward life of the individual (Lafleur, pp. 333–4). Right behaviour in a ruler is to punish malefactors and reward those who keep the law, to provide for the healing of the sick and to ensure that there is scope for those who are well to work. The head of the household is to provide for the household's needs, instruct its members and keep them from wrongdoing. The private individual, similarly, is to avoid wrong doing, do good and follow good examples (Lafleur, p. 335). So in this realm of ethics we again find lingering traces of the notion that philosophy is the guide of life.

A few ancient philosophical texts were regularly used by Christian writers on ethics in the centuries before Aristotle's *Ethics* and *Politics* became available: various Latin moralists, especially Cicero in the *De Officiis*, *De Senectute* and *De Amicitia*. Collections were made in the

Carolingian and post-Carolingian periods of moral sayings taken from classical authors.[103] Heiric of Auxerre and Sedulius Scottus did not attempt to weave these into fresh treatises in which they were subjected to Christian criticism. That was attempted by an author who may have been William of Conches, early in the twelfth century. He devised a new version of Cicero's *De Officiis* in which he says that he intends to summarise what both Cicero and Seneca say, and in which he also includes material from Horace, Terence, Lucan and Sallust. In this *Moralium Dogma Philosophorum* he explores in Ciceronian fashion but from a Christian standpoint the results of distinguishing between 'honesty' and *utilitas* in moral questions.[104] Rupert of Deutz in the same period took issue with Macrobius' account of the four virtues of prudence, temperance, fortitude and justice, on the grounds that he had no understanding of their value in the sight of God.[105] In a treatise later in the twelfth century on *The Virtues and Vices and the Gifts of the Holy Spirit*, Alan of Lille put the four virtues listed by Cicero and Macrobius alongside the faith, hope and charity of St Paul and asked how they are related to one another.[106]

Peter Abelard's *Scito te ipsum* (*Know Thyself*) was altogether a more substantial enquiry, philosophically speaking, and contained original material. He explored the Aristotelian and Boethian notion that virtue is a quality or *habitus* which an individual can acquire by effort. He also contended that God sees the intention and counts that and not the act.

Before the assimilation of Aristotle's *Ethics*, ethics remained, however, a notional subject of the syllabus, divided formally into moral principles appropriate to the private individual, those needed in family life, and those for public life.[107] Aristotle's *Ethics* was available in Latin in the twelfth century, but only Books II and III, later known as the *ethica vetus*. These parts of the book provided material on happiness and virtue. In the late 1240s, Robert Grosseteste made a complete translation, with a group of Greek commentaries to go with it: notably that of Michael of Ephesus, but including material from as early as the third century and as late as the twelfth. Albert the Great provided two new Latin commentaries, and his pupil Aquinas heard him lecture on the *Ethics*. Aquinas' own reflections on the book (about 1271–2) took him some way towards making a distinction between the study of ethics as a branch of philosophy, that is, as a speculative science; and the examination of practical questions of what it is right to do. He was also anxious to set the study of ethics in the context of the rules which govern both large and small communities, and which promote order in the state and the household, as well as in the individual soul.[108] But despite its obvious attractions as a work which allowed some sophistication of philosophical treatment in the moral sciences, the *Ethics* was slow to establish itself generally as a textbook in the schools. A number of Franciscan and Dominican commentaries survive from the fourteenth and fifteenth centuries, but it never set the schools on fire as the *libri naturales* did.

The old motifs were perhaps the most persistent. Among late thirteenth-century commentators working in the Arts Faculty at Paris there was a revival, in this new arena of academic philosophy, of the notion that philosophy is a true guide of life. This proved controversial. In 1277 the 219 Theses condemned by the Bishop of Paris included several which made bold claims for philosophers. They alone are said to be wise; their study is said to be the best possible way of life. That cannot be allowed in a Christian university. There was also a continuance of interest in the four Ciceronian and Macrobian virtues in the thirteenth century. Arnulf Provincialis refers to an ancient book *On the Intellectual Virtues* – a book apparently invented by Arnulf himself – which, he says, distinguishes *intelligentia*, *sapientia* and *phronesis*. These are the degrees by which human understanding rises from a mere love for God to a passionate desire for God. They are virtues because they are the upwardly aspiring movements of the soul, and counterparts to those habits of virtue by which we rule our bodies. The regulation of the power of reasoning produces prudence and justice; the regulation of anger produces fortitude; the regulation of desire, temperance (Lafleur, pp. 335–6).

Late mediaeval philosophy made some progress with the idea of conscience. The thirteenth-century Franciscan Bonaventure takes up earlier thinking about *synderesis* as a tendency or disposition for good, and identifies conscience as a faculty of recognition or apprehension of moral law. Aquinas agrees that *synderesis* is the natural disposition of the human mind for good which makes it possible for the conscience to act. The conscience applies the principles recognised through *synderesis*. Both Bonaventure and Aquinas see that conscience can make mistakes. Neither resorts here to Augustinian explanations in terms of the confusing effects of sin upon human reasoning. Both prefer to speak in terms of false premises and erroneous reasoning, and both are chiefly interested in the underlying questions about obligation in propositions involving 'owe' and 'ought' and 'must'. There is a shift here, perhaps, from a Platonic preoccupation with clarity and beauty and the light of right reason in the virtuous mind, to an Aristotelian interest in the mechanics of logic and language.

Philosophically speaking, politics came late to mediaeval Europe. With the end of the Roman Empire in the West, urban life as the ancient world had known it decayed even in Italy, and in northern Europe government gradually became broadly feudal. That is to say, it was tribal, run by kings and a military aristocracy which was often illiterate and dependent upon a secretariat for the production of the few documents necessary to the system: charters, treaties, letters of negotiation. Royal households were constantly on the move, using up in kind the dues of sheep and cattle and other agricultural produce owed to them by those who farmed their land. The administration of justice was not conducted in a manner which required the services of sophisticated advocates with a legal training. The essential apparatus of Greek and Roman city life had been an educated citizenry of men equipped to hold public office and regarding it as their duty to do so; a forum for public debate about matters of policy; the expectation that citizens would fight for their city when it was necessary, but that war would not be a man's career and sole serious occupation; and in Rome especially, the practice of advocacy as a routine duty of the well-born, with an education in rhetoric to teach forensic skills. Only in late mediaeval Italy did Europe produce conditions again in which something resembling this pattern was recognisable in city life.

For nearly a millennium, until Aristotle's *Politics* was translated by William of Moerbeke about 1260, the Latin West lacked textbooks from which it could have gleaned more than the sketchiest notion of the political character of this lost world. Augustine's *City of God* reflects it, but it is about many things of more immediate interest to its earlier mediaeval readers: the discussions of providence, magic, angels, heaven and hell, its summaries of classical philosophical schools of thought, for instance. Cicero's *De Officiis*, *De Amicitia*, *De Senectute*, *De Republica* gave glimpses, but his notion, for example, of civic virtue could not in the nature of things appeal on that level where it made no connection with contemporary circumstances. A literature about the ideal prince had a place in early mediaeval society, but its inspiration is not primarily philosophical. Rather, it has to do with the imitation of Christ and the exemplification of Christian virtues at their highest.

An exception to the general lack of interest in political theory before the arrival of Aristotle's *Politics* is John of Salisbury. Although he spent most of his life living in a feudal society in England and France, he writes in his *Policraticus* about the *respublica*. His chief concern was with the right to disobey or unseat a tyrant. He defines a tyrant as one who does not rule according to law; a legitimate ruler must do so. There are elements of Ciceronian thinking in his view that a *civilitas* ought to be cultivated at Court, in which love of justice balances patriotism, and the courtier is an educated man who takes pleasure in literature and conducts his life somewhat philosophically, in search of self-knowledge. But there is also a substantial influence of Christian ideals about the perfect prince in John of Salisbury's description of a monarch who is in the image of God, and of Old Testament principles on the subject of law in his account of the way rulers must remain subject to the law. (He was attacking those among his contemporaries who said on the authority of Roman law-codes that the prince is above the law.) John of Salisbury's imagery of the body public also blends classical and Christian sources.

John of Salisbury's pioneering work was not influential. Despite the groundwork he had laid, the first attempts to comment upon Aristotle's *Politics* show how uneasily it sat upon the mediaeval stomach at first (despite the comparative familiarity in the early thirteenth century of the books of the *Ethics* which deal with the virtues of good citizenship). Albert the Great found it impossible to do more than try to elucidate Aristotle's meaning. Aquinas began a commentary which was finished by Peter of Auvergne. Peter takes up what Aristotle says about kingship and adds an insistence (which would come relatively naturally to a Frenchman though perhaps less so to an Italian) that it is not merely one of the acceptable forms of government but definitely the best. Aquinas had tried to 'place' the *Politics* in a different way, by considering in his introduction to Book I what manner of science politics must be. He argues that philosophy will not be complete unless it includes a discipline which studies the city; yet the discipline is practical as well as speculative; in particular, it belongs to the moral sciences rather than the mechanical; it is the highest of the practical sciences because the city is the most important thing under the direction of human reason; moreover, it treats of the highest good in human affairs. Politics is speculative in its method. That is to say, it studies a unity, analyses it and extracts first principles. But it is also practical because it shows how the perfect city is to be brought into being and maintained.

Guy of Rimini wrote his commentary at the beginning of the fourteenth century. He had reached the stage to which commentators on Aristotle's other rediscovered writings had come almost a century earlier, of seeking to weigh Christian imperatives against the philosopher's ideas. He notes that Christians cannot wholly approve of a doctrine of natural slavery. Peter of Auvergne began the task of extracting 'questions' from the text of the *Politics*, and others followed him during the fourteenth century. That threw into relief issues the

Politics raised, for theologians as well as for those interested chiefly in making Aristotle fit mediaeval society. Is it better for a few wise men to rule, or the multitude? If the multitude should at least elect and punish princes, should they also have supreme authority to rule in general? Various considerations are brought into play: notably the question of the virtue and wisdom which those who exercise power ought to have.[109]

In the field of the theory of law we do not encounter the same long gap between the ancient world and the arousal of mediaeval interest. Law continued to be a necessity in the barbarian kingdoms which took over the Empire, and many of their rulers took over Roman codes, with modifications. From the late eleventh century there was a revival of enthusiasm for law. Ivo of Chartres in his *Panormia*, Gratian in his *Decretals* of the next generation, and a succession of school and university lawyers throughout the twelfth century and beyond turned law into an academic subject. Behind such work stood Christian assumptions: that all right and ultimately all right law comes from God; that the law of charity makes it imperative for the individual to give up his own claims to the common good. The good government operates within the framework of the whole universe under God's providence and ought to be a microcosm of it; and the just ruler is morally upright, a man of Christian virtue. Aquinas sets out a threefold hierarchy of law, in which an immutable divine law stands at the top, with a natural law beneath it which is conducive to the general human good (that a man should not be ignorant; that he should not give offence to those who live in his community with him). At the bottom comes human law, in which detailed provisions are made, in accordance with natural law, but changeable when circumstances alter (*ST* qq.93–5). The Platonic and Aristotelian categories in which early Christian thought had been so decisively cast continued to be pervasive even in the late Middle Ages. When Dante in his *De Monarchia* or Marsilius of Padua in his *Defensor Pacis* seek to begin with self-evident truths and proceed by irrefutable reasoning to their conclusions, many of the assumptions they make are those of the ancient philosophers. The notion that human society needs unity and peace to thrive seems to Dante a truth easily established if we begin from the principle that we must look for the purpose of human life on earth. He does so in Aristotelian terms. God and nature make nothing in vain. Whatever is made has a purpose or function. Created things exist not for their own existence's sake, but with an intention or end. An individual has a different purpose or function from an organised multitude of individuals. If we want to identify that collective or common purpose, we must look for the characteristic which is distinctive to the species. Only man has a capacity for intellectual growth (for the angels, which are also rational beings, do not grow in understanding). So the proper work of mankind must be to exercise this capacity. Individuals find that they grow in wisdom in tranquility. That must therefore be a necessary condition of such growth for humanity as a whole. Peace is best maintained in the community by a government which can give it unity (*De Monarchia* I.3–4). These familiar themes of the need for peace, unity, order, of human rationality and of purpose do not need to be laboured for his readers. Dante can assume their general acceptability.

Similarly, in his *Defensor Pacis*, Marsilius sets peace before us as the goal of the state. This he defines as a disposition of the state which will enable its parts to function as they ought. He therefore asks what are the causes or purposes of each part and their order in relation to one another (Discourse I.iii).

Marsilius made the experiment of seeking to demonstrate his conclusions about the temporal aspects of government by pure reason, adducing authorities in his second Discourse on the place of the Church in society (I.i.8). In the first Discourse, he considers the origin and final cause of the state in relation to its function of maintaining peace. For his account of the origins of the state, as it evolves from the single household through larger and larger assemblies of people for the common good, he is much indebted to Aristotle, in both the *Politics* and the *Nicomachean Ethics*. It is again to Aristotle that he turns for an explanation of the final cause or purpose of the state. He is much struck by Aristotle's remark in *Politics* I.i that the 'perfect community' which can live in self-sufficiency 'came into being for the sake of living well'. The state, Marsilius believes, makes it possible for mankind to live at a level beyond that of the beasts, a level fitting human dignity, in which rational beings may enjoy the exercise of their higher faculties in both thought and action (I.iv.1). But he departs from Aristotle in seeing society as created primarily by biological needs and the need for government as arising out of the human tendency to quarrel which, he argues, if unrestrained would always lead to the breakdown of society.

From this principle he derives arguments for the necessity of the state's having a series of 'parts'. There must be a standard of justice and a guardian, who sets that standard. There must be an organ of state with powers to restrain wrongdoers who offend against the standard of justice. There must be provision for various kinds of practical need, which will vary in peace and in war. There must also be provision for spiritual needs, for Marsilius' state looks to a Christian hope of the life to come, as Aristotle's could not.

Marsilius returns to Aristotle, however, when he seeks to enumerate the parts of the state more precisely (I.v). Aristotle gives him six: the agricultural, the artisan, the military, the financial, the priestly and the judicial or deliberative (*Politics* VII.8.1323^{b}2ff.). These seem to Marsilius to fall into three 'honourable' and three common functions. Only the priestly, the military and the judicial 'parts' are, he argues, strictly parts of the state; the others are necessary but at a level appropriate only to their discharge by the common people (*vulgaris*) (see also Aristotle, *Politics*, *loc. cit.*). Although he considers Aristotle's six forms of government, he comes to the conclusion that a monarchy is best, and the considerations which apply to good government for Marsilius are, again, critically different at certain points from those of Aristotle. He favours the election of the monarch by the public will. The people as a whole – or what Marsilius calls the *valentior pars* – that body of citizens which carries responsibility for the 'honourable' functions – is the legislator, or primary efficient cause of the law (I.xii). It makes law by expressing the common will in a general assembly. The monarch who is chosen to execute the law thus made must be a man of prudence and goodness, says Marsilius (I.xiv); he will have coercive power, to support which he will need an army, because there will be conflict.

Thus out of Aristotle and his own observation of human social and political behaviour and a number of Christian assumptions, Marsilius constructs a theory of secular government which rests on the assertion that the state is an expression of human rationality, designed to enable men to live according to their highest capacities as rational beings; that the chief function of political authority is to exercise control when there is conflict: it will therefore need coercive power; that the only legitimate sources of that power is the will of the people, which they express in making law and entrusting governmental authority to a monarch.

The complex questions of the relation of Church and state touches philosophy only tangentially, as Marsilius saw. But they were of great importance theologically, because they did much to shape the late mediaeval thinking about ecclesiology. In the late eleventh century, Pope Gregory VII had altered the balance of power by asserting the superiority of the spiritual over the temporal sphere. That could be defended on the authority of the so-called 'Donation of Constantine', in which the imperial power hands over a good deal to the spiritual, and which was not then discovered to be a Carolingian forgery. During the twelfth century, papal claims expanded. Bernard of Clairvaux wrote a book *On Consideration* for Eugenius III, a Pope who had once been one of his Cistercian monks. There it is argued that spiritual authority, focused in the Bishop of Rome, extends over all things on earth, and stands high in the hierarchy of heaven. A cluster of treatises of the late thirteenth and early fourteenth centuries, prompted by contemporary politics, made a contribution to this debate from the standpoint of authors with an academic training in philosophy. Dante's *De Monarchia* puts the case for the restoration of a World Emperor, a temporal 'primate' to match the spiritual, on the model of imperial Rome. John of Paris wrote *On Royal and Papal Power* in the circumstances of the encounter between Philip the Fair of France and Boniface VIII over taxation of clergy property. At stake here was the question of sovereignty. John of Paris argues (drawing heavily on Aquinas) that the Pope has no jurisdiction from Christ over the property of laymen, and thus none over temporalities. He says that the Donation of Constantine cannot be said to bind the King of France in any case; he thus provides Gallicanism with support for the view that the French Crown is independent of ecclesiastical authority in temporal affairs (and to some degree in spiritual ones, too). Most importantly perhaps for the later Middle Ages, he argues that Popes can be deposed. His grounds are that the whole Church, acting through the College of Cardinals, makes the Pope, and can therefore unmake him (24). Here we are moving towards an ecclesiology which sees the Church of the whole People of God acting by common consent, and away from the notion that the clergy, and *a fortiori* the Pope, are entrusted by God with personal power to act on behalf of the Church.

Marsilius of Padua was a radical. He argued that the Church is merely an organ of the state. He sees it as one part of the state, and a necessary one, but as standing under the coercive authority of the secular system. Its purpose is to serve the spiritual needs of the citizens and to enable them to achieve the 'sufficient life' in the world to come, as the remainder of the state's provisions make it possible for them to do in this world (Discourse II). This was a view for which he was understandably condemned by the ecclesiastical authorities, but it constituted a new and influential contribution to the long-running mediaeval debate about the respective positions of Church and state in the structures of authority.

Marsilius gave Wyclif matter for thought, as did William of Ockham (d. 1347/9), a radical among the Franciscans, who was excommunicated for his opinions. He became involved in the Church–state debate, as Marsilius did, because he was critical of the contemporary papacy. In particular, he argued for apostolic poverty and against theories of papal property-rights (a matter which had become deeply controversial during the thirteenth century); and he believed that a Pope who became a heretic was automatically stripped of his spiritual power. This doctrine involved a challenge to the contemporary view that the Pope was the final authority by which orthodoxy might be tested in matters of faith. Here, too, there was material for Wyclif to use. Wyclif himself developed out of all this a theory of dominion based on the idea that all God's faithful people possess the world and its goods in common, and must be both lord and servant to one another.

The themes of ethics and politics which caught the attention of Christian scholars above all were perhaps those of virtue and happiness. Aristotle sees the aim of the virtuous life as a human happiness which can be attained by effort and in this life (*Ethics* I.6, 1096^{b}34). (It was not always clear to his commentators that this was his message. One Paris Master of Arts of the late 1230s gave the impression in his lecture-course that Aristotle thought *beatitudo* does not need to be created; it simply exists, and a man has only to join himself to it.[110] Arnulfus Provincialis thought he could distinguish in Aristotle a double good. Virtue is attained by human effort. Felicity is not created by human efforts, but a man may join himself to it by good works.)[111]

Up to a point philosophers and Christian theologians were agreed. The end of life is happiness, and virtue is conducive to true happiness. But for the ancient philosophers this-worldly considerations necessarily had a different place from that which they occupied for Christians. Platonists might see the highest happiness as consisting in the contemplation of the Highest Good, and in freedom from the disturbances brought about by attachment to bodily pleasures (and Stoics and others could agree in part with that); but there was no exact philosophical equivalent of the Christian belief in a life to come in which happiness would be fully enjoyed and all stresses disappear. Similarly, the philosophers – here especially Aristotle – had placed an emphasis on the perfecting of the human individual which was largely in tune with Christian ideas, but with important differences as to the character of that perfection. Aristotle's perfect man is a social and political being, and a good citizen first and foremost; his virtues those which foster the well-being of the political community; Cicero's good citizen is (with Roman reservations) much the same. Augustine believed that man is not by nature a political animal, but is obliged to be so by his fall into sin, for that made it necessary for God to provide social structures and government to save him from the consequences of anarchy. Man's natural and proper citizenship when saved by grace is the citizenship of heaven. Mediaeval critics would often allow – as Godfrey of Fontaines and Henri de Gand did in the last decades of the thirteenth century – that man is at least a social if not a political animal by nature. The *perfectus homo* of Alan of Lille, writing in the Christian tradition, is above all a citizen of heaven. He is like Christ. His perfection is a freedom from sin and its consequences; the perfection of the 'philosophers' citizen' consists in being upright, balanced, reasonable and putting the common good first: an ideal which Roger Bacon and Aquinas could both endorse. Community-minded, the philosopher's good man serves his city in war or politics; the community-mindedness of the Christian is a sense of belonging to Augustine's city of heaven, the *koinonia* of the New Testament.

Anselm's descriptions of *beatitudo* encapsulate the Christian view. In the final chapters of his *Proslogion* he describes what it will be to enjoy the Highest Good, God himself. All goods of body and soul will be in that enjoyment, every innocent enjoyment known on earth in immeasurable fullness. All those who love God will be bound together in a love in which they love him and themselves and one another and God loves himself and his people through himself. There will be perfect peace, for all will will one will. Joy will abound because each will rejoice in the others' joy (25). The ladder of good things with which the *Monologion* begins, and which leads the mind and soul to the Highest Good, is in evidence here, and for Anselm earthly and bodily goods are not merely inferior things to be left behind by the soaring soul. They are for him, as for Augustine, God's creations and therefore good in themselves.

CONCLUSION

Aristotle argues in the *Posterior Analytics* that every sphere of knowledge is a distinct *disciplina* with its own first principles and rules. In the case of philosophy and theology the boundaries were repeatedly in dispute in the early Christian and mediaeval worlds, and there proved in practice to be many topics of importance to both disciplines. After the fifth and sixth centuries, Christianity tended to have the best minds in both Greek East and Latin West, and Christian scholars who did philosophy did not think of themselves first and foremost as 'philosophers'. The most original philosophical thought was in fact often Christian and theological, and that made it increasingly artificial to distinguish between the two disciplines.

Nevertheless, encounters between the two on their patches of common ground were the source of great hostility from time to time. Indeed, as we have seen, it was usually as a result of some such bruising meeting that the long-running debate about the propriety of using philosophy at all in theological investigation entered one of its active phases. That was especially noticeable in the period after the reintroduction of Aristotle's *libri naturales* into the West in the thirteenth century, when discussion shifted on to altogether more technical levels, philosophically speaking; the pretence that philosophy is theology's handmaid was hard to keep up, because almost all the important protagonists on both sides were in fact theologians.

Yet the mid-thirteenth century saw philosophy come into its own as an academic discipline in the new universities. Its independent flowering was brief, and troubled by pressing questions of its relationship to the familiar disciplines for which the syllabus already had an established place: the liberal arts and theology. By 1277 tension had escalated to a point where a series of propositions was condemned by ecclesiastical authority as incompatible with Christian orthodoxy and unsuitable

119

even for discussion in the schools. This condemnation marked a high point of crisis in the protracted story of uncomfortable relations between Christian theology and philosophy. It also threw into high relief a number of points of difficulty which had arisen during the period since Augustine made his own resolution of the problem, and which are, as we have seen, in many ways peculiarly mediaeval.

The ancient preoccupations of the scientist-philosopher with the distinction between theoretical and practical sciences persisted. There remained a sense that the theoretical was always superior to the practical, and that sciences with practical application – such as politics – were best treated theoretically, and by starting from first principles rather than observation. The triad of physics, mathematics and theology also survived, with its tendency to govern the study of physics. That did not prevent the making of some progress here, although Arabic science had a strong dominance and kept its links with its philosophical antecedents in Greek thought. Al-Khwarizmi was making a beginning in algebra as early as the ninth century, and Western mathematicians of the late Middle Ages took his work further. John Campano of Novara, in his commentary on Euclid's *Elements* of the thirteenth century, shows an awareness of the harmoniousness of the proportion later to be known as the 'Golden Section'. Nominalists pursued alternatives to classic theories of causation in the explanation of impieties. Among physicists, Peter of Spain, better known as the author of a standard textbook of logic, also worked on scientific theory in the thirteenth century. He tried to reconcile the *via experimenti* and the *via rationis*, to find a place for experimental method without disrupting the approach by reasoning. Arnold of Villanova (d. 1311) taught at Montpellier and was Court physician to the kings of Aragon and to the Pope. He made experiments, in which alchemy and magic were mixed with physics. This tendency to mix the dross of superstition with pure science was always a danger for those drawn to experimentation, and it constituted a drag on progress in the sciences for some centuries.

The end of the Middle Ages saw a changing perception of the ancient world, and of the standing of philosophy within it. From at least the fourteenth century, and arguably earlier, classical literature was beginning to be read with a fuller sense of the culture it embodied, and not only as a treasury of snippets which could be borrowed to illustrate or support an argument. The philosophical literature stood alongside those of history and poetry in this movement. Cicero's oratory and his philosophy could alike be read for their style as well as their content. It cannot perhaps be said that the first humanists had a wholly clear or indeed objective picture of the ancient world. There is evidence of some romanticism about *Romanitas*, and a sense that the classical period had been a golden age of thought and expression to which the moderns could only aspire wistfully to return. Juan Luis Vives, for example, one of the Paris scholars at the beginning of the sixteenth century, assumed like many humanists of the period that the people who first used Latin decided what is good usage. There was no real sense of the evolution of language, the process by which new patterns of speech become in their turn good style. Melanchthon (following Quintilian) saw a word as something like a coin. It must not be a forgery. It must be true to its value. It must be passed from the user to those who use it after him, preserving the true 'value' it originally had.

The urge to go back to origins was matched in other areas. Students of the Bible began to seek out manuscripts of the Greek and Hebrew texts, in an endeavour to return to the *fontes*, and the study of Greek in particular began to open up more fully than ever before in the West since the end of the Roman world a sense of the character of ancient Greek culture and thought. In imitation of a perceived classical ideal, the educated man strove to be a Renaissance man, cultured rather than learned, perhaps (*cultus* rather than *doctus*), urbane, sophisticated; and inclined to sneer at the mechanical laboriousness of the scholastic method and to regard the Latin language in the form used in late mediaeval scholasticism as barbarous and debased.

Paradoxically, all this had the effect of moderating the often uncritical respect in which the ancient *auctores* had commonly been held throughout the Middle Ages. The new scholarship inclined its adherents to think of making mistakes. That should be contrasted with Bernard of Chartres's famous dictum of the twelfth century, that even the greatest scholars of his own day were but as dwarfs sitting on the shoulders of the giants of old, so that even if they could perhaps see further than their predecessors, that was only because they had been lifted up so high on the 'shoulders' of their great work. Lorenzo Valla, in the fourteenth century, speaks of Priscian and Porphyry as fellow mortals to be criticised for their scholarly failings like any contemporary. Rudolph Agricola argues that 'Aristotle was a man of supreme intelligence, learning, eloquence, knowledge and wisdom; but still he was only a man'. Erasmus felt free to point out slips made by Hilary of Poitiers or Augustine, for they were 'very great men, but only men after all'.

These trends, growing increasingly strong with the fifteenth and early sixteenth centuries, ran alongside a steady continuance in the familiar mediaeval ways. Indeed, in some universities in late fifteenth-century Germany, courses in new humanist work were conducted on the fringes of the syllabus. For some decades two types of textbook of grammar and logic were being produced: the old and the new, technically simplified, which claimed to cut through all the dead wood and present the essentials. Peter Ramus' reworking of Aristotle is perhaps the most influential of these. Universities, such as Wittenberg in the first half of the sixteenth century, which took a lead in the teaching of Greek and encouraged the new approach to the teaching of grammar and logic, can still be found conducting *disputationes* in the late mediaeval way, in the middle of the century. Scholasticism was noisily rejected by protestant scholarship in the sixteenth century and after, although its methods continued (and to some degree still continue) in use in the Roman Catholic tradition of scholarship. In practice it was some generations before the influence of late mediaeval approaches died away in protestant communities too. We find Luther reintroducing formal academic disputations at Wittenberg in the 1530s, and similar disputations being conducted at the trials of Ridley and others in England. The use of *loci communes*, or 'articles', was pervasive among reformers when drawing up confessions of faith; and these were, after all, nothing but the *theses* of mediaeval academic debate. The result was a conscious contrasting of approaches to the heritage of ancient learning, a sense of new ground being broken and of rebirth.

The influx of Aristotelian logic and science in the last mediaeval centuries had now been absorbed into a system of explanation of the universe and its running which had become common doctrine. Order is seen as a safeguard against conflict and the ultimate dissolution of all things into chaos. That is as true for the ordering of the natural world as for the ordering of human society. Peace, harmony, changelessness are as much the highest good here as they were for the first Platonists. All this can be said without reference to sin, and the Christian teaching that it is from sin that all disorder arises; on the other hand, there is no conflict with Christian theology in these assumptions. Hierarchy is a concomitant of this system. The very elements, fire, air, earth and water, are ranged in their places in the world. All created things have their position and purpose, the lower to meet the needs of the higher. Just as, among the vegetables, trees stand higher than small plants, so in human society some are born to rule, others to serve. 'It may not be called order except it do contain it in degrees, high and base, according to the merit or estimation of the thing that is ordered', comments the English Elizabethan Elyot, in the first chapter of his book *The Governor*.

In theology, the late Middle Ages saw new preoccupations. The old areas of common ground with philosophy were not abandoned. Questions about being and substance and the powers of knowledge of intellectual beings were not neglected; indeed, their treatment reached new heights of subtlety. But contemporary events made ecclesiology interesting. The Conciliarist movement and papal resistance to attempts to moderate claims to pontifical plenitude of power drew attention in the fourteenth and fifteenth centuries to theories about decision-making in the Church. The theology of the sacraments, particularly in the area of the Eucharist, penance and indulgences, was also developing; under the challenge of Luther and his contemporaries, it was to become a principal focus of attention for much of the sixteenth century. In both areas, problems of authority in the Church arose with unprecedented intensity, in areas to which ancient philosophy could make a contribution only at the level of the most fundamental questions of methodology.

In the doctrine of man there had been, from the twelfth century, a 'discovery of the individual'.[1] Earlier mediaeval literature, like that of the ancient world, describes the typical representative of a 'class' of the good or the brave, the wicked or the foolish, the virtuous citizen, the benevolent ruler, the philosopher, and so on. Saints' lives by the end of the eleventh century were often written by hired hagiographers, who endowed their subjects with the requisite qualities, sometimes regardless of any real personal differences between them in life. That began to change.

In their concern with the perennial topics of philosophical discussion since the Greeks, mediaeval theologians kept alive the classical tradition. But indubitably, they did more in some areas. They enlarged the scope and technical possibilities of Aristotle's logic. They penetrated much further than Aristotle or the Roman grammarians had done into the nature and behaviour of natural languages. They refined both vocabulary and concept in speaking of divine 'being'. They introduced philosophical categories into the discussion of Church and sacraments. They created an enormous corpus of new work of the utmost subtlety and inventiveness. Some of their work is of a great deal more than antiquarian interest today, especially in the area of the philosophy of language.

Perhaps we can say, above all, that philosophical theology remained alive and growing for a thousand years as a result of mediaeval efforts, and that in this way it transmitted a heritage not by burying the talent it was given but by putting it to use and multiplying it. And it is of no small importance that it was out of the cataclysmic fresh juxtaposition of mediaeval and ancient world-pictures in the sixteenth century that modern theology and philosophy sprang.

NOTES

1 PHILOSOPHY AND THEOLOGY

1 On the Greek-speaking East, see *CHLGEMP*, Part VI.

2 See P. Courcelle, 'Étude critique sur les commentaires de Boèce (ixe–xve siècles)', *AHDLMA* (1939), 5–40, 53, and T. Gregory, *Platonismo medievale* (Rome, 1958), pp. 1–15. Adalbold, Bishop of Utrecht (d. 1026), takes that view in his commentary and is able to see Boethius as a Christian philosopher.

3 In Aquinas' day, 'the Philosopher' was normally Aristotle.

4 See J. Swanson, *John of Wales* (Cambridge, 1989), pp. 167ff. on the imitation of the virtues of the philosophers.

5 *The Works of Gilbert Crispin*, ed. A. S. Abulafia and G. R. Evans (London, 1986), pp. 61–2.

6 *Dialogus inter Philosophum, Iudaeum et Christianum*, ed. R. Thomas (Stuttgart, 1970), p. 41.

7 See R. W. Southern, *St Anselm and his Biographer* (Cambridge, 1963).

8 *Dialogus, op. cit.*, p. 90.

9 *Ibid.*, p. 98.

10 Swanson, *op. cit.*, p. 172.

11 See my *Old Arts and New Theology* (Oxford, 1978) for examples.

12 Arnulf describes various ways in which philosophy can be divided. Its speculative branch is concerned with the causes of things; its practical with the student's manner of life, and how to avoid vices and cultivate virtues. Or one may say that philosophy has three branches: natural science, mathematics and the study of the divine. These are of its essence, although it may touch on a variety of accidental matters, such as language and virtue. Or, if philosophy is taken to include all knowledge which meets human needs, it can be divided into the liberal arts (which serve the soul's needs) and the mechanical arts (which serve those of the body) (Lafleur, pp. 314–17).

   Beside Arnulf's list might be set those of several of his contemporaries. One, writing about 1230–40, suggests that the final cause of philosophy is the knowledge of all that is; its efficient cause, man's complete knowledge of himself, its material cause, the knowledge of divine and human matters together with the principles of right living; its formal cause, assimilation to the Creator by human virtue. Another, also anonymous, writing perhaps five years before Arnulf, gives, in a less contrived framework, a selection of the definitions Arnulf cites (see Lafleur, pp. 181, 258). Alternative arrangements of the same elements are also found: a division into mechanical and liberal studies in which *philosophia liberalis* is divided into speculative (the arts of language) and practical (the cultivation of virtue) (Lafleur, p. 18). This is with respect to the 'knower'. With respect to the 'knowledge' and the manner in which it may be 'knowable', a division between *theoretica* and *practica* is proposed. The first 'knows' the substance of things by their universal causes; the second knows their 'qualities' or modes of operating, and that is practica (Lafleur, p. 183). 'Natural philosophy' is sometimes simply given its Aristotelian and Boethian division into physics, mathematics and metaphysics or theology (Lafleur, pp. 183–4 and 261). Elsewhere we find philosophy grouped with *mechanica* and *magica* under *humana scientia*, and set over against *theologia*, which is the *divina scientia* (Lafleur, p. 259).

13 Jean Gerson, *De Erroribus circa Artem Magicam* (1402), *Oeuvres complètes*, X (Paris, 1973), p. 78.

14 *Ibid.*

15 *Ibid.*, p. 79.

16 *Ibid.*, p. 81.

17 *Ibid.*, pp. 85–6.

18 Gerson, *Trilogium Astrologiae Theologiatae* (1419), *Oeuvres complètes*, X, p. 90.

19 See H. Chadwick, *Boethius* (Oxford, 1981), p. 110.

20 Jean Gerson, *Oeuvres complètes*, IX (Paris, 1973), pp. 188–90.

21 William of Auxerre, *Summa Aurea*, ed. J. Ribaillier (Paris/Rome, 1980), *Spicilegium Bonaventurianum*, XVI, p. 15, and see J. de Ghellinck, *Le Mouvement théologique du xii* siècle (Brussels/Paris, 1948), pp. 279–84 on I Peter 3.15.

22 William of Auxerre, *op. cit.*, p. 16.

23 *Ibid.*, pp. 18ff.

24 *Ibid.*, p. 17.

25 R. Holte, *Béatitude et sagesse* (Paris, 1962), p. 97.

26 *Chartularium Universitatis Parisiensis*, I.47–8, in L. Thorndike, *University Records* (New York, 1944), no. 11, p. 22.

27 M. Grabmann, 'I divieti ecclesiastici di Aristotele sotto Innocenzo III e Gregorio IX', *Miscellanea Historiae Pontificiase*, 5 (1941), 83.

28 G. Post, 'Philosophantes and Philosophi', *AHDLMA* (1954), 135–8.

29 *Contra Quatuor Labyrinthos Franciae*, ed. P. Glorieux, *AHDLMA* (1952), 270ff.

30 'La Somme "Quoniam homines" d'Alain de Lille', ed. P. Glorieux, *AHDLMA* (1952), 119 and cf. J. Leclerq, 'Un témoignage du xiii siècle sur la nature de la théologie', *AHDLMA* (1942), 301–21.

31 *CHLMP*, p. 89.

32 *Ibid.*, p. 91.

33 Roger Bacon, *Metaphysica*, ed. R. Steele, *Opera Hactenus Inedita*, I (London, 1905, p. 1) and *Compendium Studii Theologiae*, ed. H. Rashdall (Aberdeen, 1911), p. 25.

34 Ed. J. Koch and J. O. Riedl (Milwaukee, 1944).

35 See R. Hissette, *Enquête sur les 219 Articles condamnés à Paris le 7 Mars 1277* (Paris, 1977).

36 See Jerome, *Letter* 22, *Select Letters*, ed. F. A. Wright (London, 1933), pp. 126-7.
37 'I divieti', 61 and see E. Warichez, *Etienne de Tournai et son temps, 1128–1203* (Tournai/Paris, 1936), p. 91.
38 'I divieti', 63 and G. Lacombe, *Prepositini Cancellarii Parisiensis, 1206–10, Opera Omnia, Bibliothèque Thomiste*, XI (Paris, 1927), pp. 41ff.
39 'I divieti', 72.
40 See Holte, *Béatitude et sagesse*, p. 180.
41 'I divieti', 76.
42 *Ibid.*
43 'I divieti', 79.

2 PHILOSOPHICAL SOURCES

1 See, for example, R. B. C. Huygens, *Accessus ad Auctores* (Lieden, 1970).
2 M. Grabmann, *I divieti ecclesiastici di Aristotele sotto Innocenzio III e Gregorio IX, Miscellanea Historiae Pontificiae*, 7 (Rome, 1941), p. 6.
3 G. Théry, 'Autour du décret de 1210, I, David de Dinant', *Bibliothèque Thomiste*, VI (Le Saulchoire, 1925), pp. 7ff.
4 G. Leff, *Paris and Oxford Universities in the Thirteenth and Fourteenth Centuries* (New York, 1968), p. 192.
5 *Logica Modernorum*, ed. L. M. de Rijk (2 vols., Assen, 1971) has excellent indexes of stock questions treated by the logicians.
6 See J. W. Baldwin, *Masters, Princes and Merchants* (Princeton, 1970), on the number of Masters teaching theology at the end of the twelfth century.
7 Théry, *op. cit.*
8 *I divieti*, pp. 10–14.
9 *Ibid.*, p. 101.
10 *Ibid.*, pp. 72ff.
11 *Ibid.*, p; 95.
12 *Ibid.*, p. 101.
13 L. Thorndike, *University Records* (New York, 1944), no. 20.
14 'I divieti', p. 92.
15 Thorndike, p. 64.
16 *Ibid.*, p. 47.
17 P. Mandonnet, *Siger of Brabant et l'Averroîsme latin au xiiiᵉ siècle* (Louvain, 1911), pp. 90ff.
18 Ockham, *Tractatus de Quantitate, Opera Theologica*, X (New York, 1986), ed. C. Grassi, pp. 5–6.
19 *Chartularium universitatis Parisiensis*, I.586–7, and cf. Ludovicus Coronel, *Perscrutationes physicales* (Lyons, 1530, written 1506–11), fols. xciiᵛ–xciiiʳ, Thorndike, *University Records*, p. 87.
20 There is evidence, for example, that Lanfranc of Bec, who taught Anselm, may have known it.
21 *De Universo* (1674), Iⁱⁱ, 14; 1, p. 821b.
22 Venice, MS Marciana 2492, fol. 124r.
23 The term 'Organon' for the six books of Aristotle's logic seems to have come into use in the sixteenth century.

24 Some in a spirit of scientific curiosity (Adelard of Bath), some in an attempt to translate the Koran into Latin so that Moslems might be converted to Christianity (the party sent out by Peter the Venerable, abbot of Cluny).
25 A Jew living in Arab territory.
26 See R. W. Southern, *Robert Grosseteste* (Oxford, 1986).
27 See *Aristoteles Latinus*, ed. L. Minio-Paluello (Oxford, 1972), XXVI.2 and especially pp. cxlii–cxlvii.
28 See *CHLMP*, pp. 51–2.
29 Most important of all perhaps to Augustine was the now lost *Hortensius*. See *Confessions* III.iv.
30 See H. Silvestre, 'Note sur la survie de Macrobe au moyen âge', *Classica et medievalia*, 24 (1963), 170–80.
31 This material also found a place in the Cabbala, the theosophic Jewish mysticism which appeared in the mid-twelfth century. See G. Vadja, 'Un chapitre de l'histoire du conflit entre la Kabbale et la philosophie', *AHDLMA* (1955), 45–144.
32 See A. Badawi, *Histoire de la philosophie en Islam* (Paris, 1972), 385–477.
33 See 'Al-Kindi, *De Radiis*', ed. M. T. d'Alverny and F. Hudry, *AHDLMA* (1974), 139–260.

3 KNOWING AND LANGUAGE

1 Cf. Plotinus, *Ennead* V.9.6.1–10.
2 On self-evidence, see p. 43ff.
3 *Summa Aurea* (1500, reprinted Frankfurt, Minerva, 1964), III.3, c.2, q.3, fol. 135ʳ1.
4 See D. P. Henry, *The Logic of St. Anselm* (Oxford, 1967), pp. 207–8, for a discussion.
5 So Porphyry says in his Commentary on Aristotle's *Categories* (ed. A. Busse, 1887, *Commentaria in Aristotelem Graeca* IV.1, p. 91).
6 *Logica Modernorum*, ed. L. M. de Rijk (Assen, 1967), IIⁱ.113–17 and 123–5.
7 In Roman grammatical theory the adjective is classed with the noun.
8 Ed. G. Friedlein (Leipzig, 1867), p. 5.5–7.
9 Adelard of Bath made translations of the *Elements*.
10 See *CHLMP*, p. 115.
11 G. Raynaud de Lage, 'Deux questions sur la foi inspirées d'Alain de Lille', *AHDLMA* (1943–5), 322–36.
12 Aquinas, *Quodlibet* VII. q.6.a.1.
13 See my *Alan of Lille* (Cambridge, 1983).
14 R. Bacon, *Compendium Studii Theologiae*, ed. H. Rashdall (Aberdeen, 1911), p. 25.

4 GOD

1 *De Lib. Arb.* II.25–54.
2 Plotinus, *Enneads* V.3 [49] 14.6–7.
3 For references, see *CHLGMP*, pp. 469, 494, 497. See, too, Anselm, *Monologion*, 26, on the idea that God is outside and above every 'substance' if we take the word 'substance' in any ordinary sense.
4 *Proslogion, Proemium*.

5 J. Paulus, 'Les Disputes d'Henri de Gand et de Gilles de Rome sur la distinction de l'essence et de l'existence', *AHDLMA* (1942), 23–358.
6 Giles of Rome, *Theoremata de esse et essentia*, ed. E. Hocedez (Louvain, 1930), and tr. M. V. Murray (Milwaukee, 1952), Introduction discusses these views.
7 *Proslogion*, I.
8 See C. F. Kelley, *Meister Eckhart on Divine Knowledge* (Yale, 1977), pp. 60ff.
9 It is perhaps worth remarking on the debt to Anselm here.
10 A. Hayen, 'Le Concile de Reims et l'erreur théologique de Gilbert de la Porrée', *AHDLMA* (1935), 56.
11 Gilbert of Poitiers, *Commentaries on Boethius*, ed. N. M. Häring (Toronto, 1966), p. 98.63.
12 *Ibid.*, p. 90.35.
13 S 1.228.25–8.
14 S 1.282.28–32.
15 S 1.283.1–6.
16 Aquinas, *Quodlibet* VII. q.iii.a.i.

5 THE COSMOS

1 Aquinas, *Quodlibet* V.9.q.1.a.1.
2 R. C. Dales, 'Henricus de Harclay, Questio "Utrum mundus potuit fuisse ab eterno"', *AHDLMA* (1983), 223–55.
3 *CHLGEMP*, p. 478.
4 P. Hadot, 'Marius Victorinus et Alcuin', *AHDLMA* (1955), 5–19.
5 See B. Stock, *Myth and Science in the Twelfth Century* (Princeton, 1972), pp. 119–23.
6 Cf. *CHLMP*, pp. 497ff.
7 See Proclus, *Elements of Theology*, ed. and tr. E. R. Dodds, p. 251; Augustine, *Confessions* VI.3.
8 See *Roger Bacon's Philosophy of Nature*, ed. D. C. Lindberg (Oxford, 1983), pp. xxxi–xii.
9 See R. A. Markus, 'Augustine: Reason and Illumination', in *CHLGEMP*.
10 Lindberg, *op. cit.*, p. xlix.
11 Avencebrol (Ibn Gebirol), *Fons Vitae*, ed. C. Baeumker, *BGPM*, i.2–7 (Münster, 1895), pp. 106–8, for example.
12 E.g. *De Docta Ignorantia* II.4 (116.17–19).
13 See, too, p. 69ff. on the *regio dissimilitudinis*.
14 Alan of Lille, *Regulae Theologiae*, ed. Häring, notes 50, 71.
15 Dodds, *ed. cit.*, Proposition 98, p. 87; see also the Latin *Liber de Causis*, ed. O. Bardenhewer (Freiburg i.B., 1882), pp. 168–9.
16 N. M. Häring, 'The Creation and Creator of the World according to Thierry of Chartres and Clarembald of Arras', *AHDLMA* (1955), 137–216.
17 H. A. Oberman and J. A. Weishiepl, 'Sermo Epicinius, ascribed to Thomas Bradwardine (1346)', *AHDLMA* (1958), 295–329.
18 Aquinas, *Quodlibet* V.q.2.a.1. Alan of Lille, *Summa Quoniam Homines*, 86, pp. 230–1.
19 *Quodlibets* (Louvain, 1546), p. 4.
20 Cf. Alan of Lille, *Summa Quoniam Homines*, 85, p. 230; Aquinas, *Quodlibet* V.q.2.a.2.

21 S. Runciman, *The Mediaeval Manichee* (Cambridge, 1947), discusses whether continuity can be traced from the late antique to the mediaeval communities of these heretics.

22 See F. Châtillon, '*Regio dissimilitudinis*', in *Mélanges F. Podechard* (Lyon, 1945), p. 99; A. E. Taylor, '*Regio dissimilitudinis*', *AHDLMA* (1934), 305–6; P. Courcelle, 'Tradition neo-platonicienne et traditions chrétiennes de la "region de dissemblance" (Plato, *Politique*, 273ᵈ)', *AHDLMA* (1957), 5–33.

23 Peter Abelard pursued this point a little further. See *Pietro Abelardo scritti di logica*, ed. M. dal Pra (1969), p. 103 *et al.*

24 *Summa Quoniam Homines* 106, p. 241.

25 See, too, *CHLMP*, pp. 367ff.

26 See H. Chadwick, *Augustine* (Oxford, 1986), for a summary.

27 Ed. G. Madec, *CCCM* (1978).

28 These authors are discussed in O. Lottin, *Psychologie et morale aux xiiᵉ et xiiiᵉ siècles* (2nd edn, Gembloux, 1957), I.67ff.

29 *Ibid.*, V.29–34.

30 H. Dondaine, 'Les "Expositiones super Ierarchiam Caelestem" de Jean Scot Eriène', *AHDLMA* (1950), 245–302.

31 In *Somn. Scip.* I.10.7–16.

32 Aquinas, *In Libros Aristotelis de Caelo et Mundo Expositio, Opera Omnia* (Vatican, 1889), 3, 186ff., II Lect. 17 and cf. *ST* I.q.32.a.1.

33 Bonaventure, *Itinerarium Mentis ad Deum*, ed. W. Hover (München, 1970), II.2.

34 *Ibid.*

35 *Ibid.*, II.10.

36 *Ibid.*, I.2, 14.

6 MAN

1 William of Auxerre, *Summa Aurea* IV.547.

2 *Quodlibet* III.q.8.a.1.

3 *Quodlibet* I.q.7.a.1.

4 A. Moody, *Studies in Mediaeval Philosophy, Science and Logic* (California, 1975), p. 40.

5 *Quodlibet* III.q.9.a.1.

6 H. Chadwick, in *Harvard Theological Review*, 41 (1948), 94ff.

7 Ps.-Byrhtferth on Bede, *De Natura Rerum*, *PL* 90.190–1.

8 *PL* 150.411.

9 *Ibid.*

10 Lottin, p. 190.

11 *Essentialiter et vere*, for example, instead of *substantialiter et vere* (*PL* 180.885); *essentia Dominici corporis* in Lanfranc (*PL* 150.430); both *naturaliter* and *substantialiter* in Durandus (*PL* 149.392 and 1386 and 'ex visibilibus et terrenis substantiis, id est panis et vino . . . sanctum Domini corpus ac verus sanguis efficitur, mutata non specie sed natura' (*PL* 149.1380). This usage takes the notion of 'substance' out of the realm of the tangible and allows for spiritual and divine substance without any difficulty.

12 *PL* 180.349–50.

13 *PL* 180.791.

14 'Nec album efficit albedo illa, nec rotundum rotunditas illa', *PL* 180.343.

15 *PL* 180.350.
16 Lottin, p. 278.
17 *PL* 150.430.
18 Lottin, pp. 27, 55.
19 Lottin, p. 217.
20 Simon of Tournai, *Disputationes*, ed. J. Warichez, *SSlov.*, 12 (1932), p. 202, Disp. 71, q.4, p. 258, Disp. 90, q.2; p. 259, Disp. 90, q.3.
21 *Sententie Parisienses, Ecrits de l'école d'Abélard*, ed. A. Landgraf, *SSlov.*, 14 (1934), p. 40.
22 'Non . . . subducto pane et supposito corpore Christi.'
23 Robert of Melun, on I Corinthians 10.16, p. 210.
24 Master Simon, *De Sacramentis*, ed. H. Weisweilber, *SSlov.* 17 (1937), p. 30 and pp. CXXXI and CLI.
25 Simon of Tournai, p. 202, Disp. 71, q.5.
26 *PL* 210.678.
27 *PL* 149.1430.
28 *CCCM* 22.647, on Exodus 2.10.
29 *PL* 180.739.
30 'Si dici posset, diceretur impanatum', *PL* 180.342.
31 *PL* 180.431–2.
32 'Sicut Verbum fit caro, sic panis fit eadem caro', *PL* 180.755.
33 *PL* 180.755.
34 *Ibid.*
35 *PL* 180.754.
36 'Similis quidem est grammatica, sed non similis intelligentia', *PL* 180.754.
37 *PL* 180.754.
38 Ibid.
39 Lottin, p. 217.
40 *PL* 180.343.
41 *Ut absque substantia subsistat efficere, Ysagoge in Theologiam*, Ecrits de l'école d'Abélard, p. 203.
42 *Master Simon*, Appendix, containing Petrus Manducator's text, in Robert of Melun, *In Epistolas Pauli*, ed. R. Martin, *Spicilegium Sacrum Lovaniense* 18 (1938), p. 53, and see opening discussion on the treatment of this aspect in the mid-twelfth century.
43 *PL* 180.362.
44 *Ibid.*
45 p. 124.
46 Gilbert, p. 128; Durandus, *PL* 149.1401.
47 'Aliqua inter catholicos questio est', Lottin, p. 132.
48 'Qualis ipse naturaliter fuit', Lottin, p. 132; see also many other examples, e.g. Lottin, pp. 217–19).
49 Simon of Tournai, p. 200, Disp. 71, q.1; Lottin, pp. 105–6.
50 'Totus ferebat se ipsum et totus ferebatur a se in manibus suis', says Gilbert, p. 129.
51 *PL* 149.1450.
52 Huygens, p. 204 and frequently elsewhere.
53 *PL* 180.783.
54 *PL* 149.1402–3.
55 p. 129.

56 *Ibid.*
57 *PL* 180.780.
58 *PL* 150.439.
59 'Ista excedunt corpore naturam substantie', p. 129.
60 E.g. William of St Thierry, *PL* 180.346–7.
61 *PL* 149.1431.
62 *PL* 149.1430.
63 *PL* 149.1432.
64 *PL* 149.1377.
65 Lottin, p. 218.
66 *PL* 149.1458.
67 *PL* 149.1384.
68 *PL* 149.1382.
69 *PL* 180.747 and 885.
70 Lottin, p. 28. Rupert of Deutz, *CCCM*, XXIV, p. 1832, and Robert of Melun, *Quaestiones de divina pagina, SSlov.*, 13 (1932), p. 22, q.38.
71 Gilbert, p. 132; Alger, *PL* 180.798; Lottin, p. 279, for example.
72 Durand, *PL* 149.1382; Alger, *PL* 180.803; Lottin, p. 280; Robert of Melun, *Quaestiones de divinia pagina*, p. 22, q.38.
73 *PL* 150.420.
74 *PL* 149.1397.
75 *PL* 180.883–4.
76 Lottin, p. 28; Robert of Melun, on I Corinthians 10.16, p. 210; *Sententie Parisienses*, p. 40.
77 *PL* 149.1430.
78 *PL* 149.1380.
79 *PL* 149.1385.
80 Gilbert, p. 127.
81 *Ibid.*, p. 126.
82 'Sub eadem verborum prolatione sint dicta'. *Ibid.*
83 Gilbert, p. 126.
84 *Ibid.*
85 Alger, *PL* 180.755.
86 *PL* 180.756.
87 *PL* 180.852. See my *The Logic and Language of the Bible*, I (Cambridge, 1984), pp. 101–22.
88 'Haec autem verba ad aliquid sunt', *PL* 150.436.
89 *PL* 150.436; cf. Alger, *PL* 180.791, also on confusion of words and *ad aliquid*.
90 See, in particular, Durandus, *PL* 149.1400.
91 *Consueto sacrorum codicum more*.
92 *PL* 150.438.
93 See especially the *Final Report* of the Anglican-Roman Catholic International Commission, 1981, *Eucharist* (6), note 2: 'The word "transubstantiation" is commonly used in the Roman Catholic Church to indicate that God acting in the Eucharist effects a change in the inner reality of the elements. The term should be seen as affirming the fact of Christ's presence and of the mysterious and radical change which takes place. In contemporary Roman Catholic theology it is not understood as explaining how the change takes place.'

94 p. 127.
95 *PL* 149.1457.
96 *PL* 149.1393.
97 *PL* 180.775.
98 *PL* 150.430.
99 *Ibid.*
100 *PL* 180.758–9.
101 *PL* 149.1445.
102 Ysgoge, p. 203, and Master Simon, p. 90.
103 E.g. C. H. Talbot, *Florilegium morale Oxoniense, Analecta Medievalia, Namurcensia*, VI (1956), 12–13; and R. Quadri, *I Collectanea di Eirico di Auxerre, Spicilegium Friburgense*, XI (Freiburg, 1966).
104 William of Conches, *Moralium Dogma Philosophorum*, ed. J. Holberg (Uppsala, 1929).
105 *PL* 168.1401–3, *De Gloria et Honorius Filii Hominis*.
106 *Textes inédits d'Alain de Lille*, ed. M. T. d'Alverny (Paris, 1965), pp. 61–4.
107 See the twelfth-century schemata.
108 See R. A. Gautier, 'Cours sur l'Ethica Nova', *AHDLMA* (1975), 141.
109 Cf. P. de L'apparent, 'L'Oeuvre politique de François de Mayronnes, ses rapports avec celle de Dante', *AHDLMA* (1940), 5–152.
110 R. A. Gauthier, 'Le Cours sur l'*Ethica Nova* d'un maitre ès arts de Paris (1235–40)', *AHDLMA* (1975), 71–141.
111 R. A. Gauthier, 'Arnoul de Provence et la doctrine de la fronesis', *Revue du moyen âge latin*, 19 (1963), 139.

CONCLUSION

1 C. Morris, *The Discovery of the Individual* (London, 1972).

FURTHER READING

TEXTS

The classical source-texts are conveniently accessible in the Loeb series, with Latin or Greek facing the English translation. For mediaeval authors the position is more mixed. References are given in the text for a number of these, but although Anselm of Canterbury is translated in full by J. Hopkins and H. Richardson (4 vols, New York, Edwin Mellen Press, 1976), and Aquinas is available in a number of English versions, many of them are still not to be had in English translation or, in some cases, in modern editions.

GENERAL HISTORIES

The Cambridge History of Later Greek and Earlier Medieval Philosophy, ed. A. H. Armstrong (Cambridge, Cambridge University Press, 1970)
The Cambridge History of Later Medieval Philosophy, ed. N. Kretzmann, A. Kenny and J. Pinborg (Cambridge, Cambridge University Press, 1982)
Both these contain extensive bibliographies on particular authors and movements.
Medieval Jewish Philosophy, ed. S. T. Katz (New York, Arno Press, 1980)
Evans, G. R., *Old Arts and New Theology* (Oxford, Oxford University Press, 1980)
Leaman, O., *An Introduction to Medieval Islamic Philosophy* (Cambridge, Cambridge University Press, 1985)
Marenbon, J., *Later Medieval Philosophy* (London, Routledge, 1987)
—— *Early Medieval Philosophy* (London, Routledge, 1988)

OTHER MODERN WORKS

Chadwick, H., *Boethius* (Oxford, 1981)
Henry, D. P., *The Logic of St. Anselm* (Oxford, 1967)
Kelley, C. F., *Meister Eckhart on Divine Knowledge* (Yale, 1977)
Leff, G., *Paris and Oxford Universities in the Thirteenth and Fourteenth Centuries* (New York, 1968)
Lindberg, D. C., ed., *Roger Bacon's Philosophy of Nature* (Oxford, 1983)
Moody, A., *Studies in Mediaeval Philosophy, Science and Logic* (California, 1975)

FURTHER READING

Rudavsky, *Divine Omniscience and Omnipotence in Medieval Philosophy* (Dordrecht, Reidel, 1984)
Swanson, J., *John of Wales* (Cambridge, 1989)
Thorndike, L., *University Records* (New York, 1944)

INDEX

7282

189 Ev 1
Evans, G. R.
Philosophy and theology in
 the Middle Ages

DEC 16 '06	DATE DUE		

Nyack College Library
Nyack, NY 10960